SHAKES

Shakespeare in China

MURRAY J. LEVITH

continuum

CONTINUUM
The Tower Building, 11 York Road, London SE1 7NX
80 Maiden Lane, Suite 704, New York, NY 10038

www.continuumbooks.com

First published 2004
Paperback edition 2006

British Library Cataloguing-in-Publication Data
*A catalogue record for this book is available
from the British Library*

ISBN 0 8264 6137 9 (hardback)
ISBN 0 8264 9276 2 (paperback)

Typeset by RefineCatch Limited, Bungay, Suffolk
Printed and bound in Great Britain by
Biddles Ltd., King's Lynn, Norfolk

And again, for Tina

Contents

Acknowledgements

The faculty of the University of Birmingham's Shakespeare Institute, Stratford-upon-Avon, elected me a 'Visiting Fellow' in 2001 which enabled me to complete this long-standing project. The Shakespeare Institute Library, the Shakespeare Centre Library, the Folger Shakespeare Library, and the Skidmore College Library were all most helpful as I did my research. I should especially like to acknowledge Amy Syrell and Marilyn Sheffer, the inter-library loan people in the Scribner Library at Skidmore College, and Dr Susan Brock of the Shakespeare Centre Library. Dr Jason Gleckman, of the Chinese University of Hong Kong, tracked down a crucial study for me and deserves special thanks as well. My colleague and good friend Professor Mason Y.H. Wang helped in ways too numerous to mention and over a period of many years. And, of course, Skidmore College for their past and continuing support.

Various universities and organizations allowed me to present parts of this study in a number of lectures and seminars. These include Qufu Teachers University (People's Republic of China), the University of Petroleum–China (People's Republic of China), the Chinese University of Hong Kong, Tamkang University (Taiwan), University of Durban–Westville (South Africa), the Australian/New Zealand Shakespeare Association, the Shakespeare Association of America, and the South Central

Acknowledgements

Modern Language Association (United States). Earlier versions of two of my chapters have seen print. Thanks to the University of Western Australia Press and *The Shakespeare Newsletter* for allowing their inclusion here.

There are many individuals to acknowledge. Some provided articles and books, helped with bibliographies and translations, read drafts, made suggestions, offered corrections, or simply encouraged the study along. Chen Mao, Birgit Linder, Qiu Ke'an, Cao Yafei, Zhou Mei, Michael Shapiro, Alan Wheelock, Nanette Jaynes, Jim Shaw, Helen Hargest, and Yang Lingui. James Croft was my careful copy editor at Continuum. Additionally, I could not have written this book without the studies of scholars who have come before me, especially Li Ruru, He Qixin, Meng Xianqiang, Zhang Xiaoyang, Ching-Hsi Perng, Dorothy Wong, and David S.P. Yang. My aim was to add new information to their pioneering work and provide Western readers a guide to Shakespeare in the Chinas in the twentieth century.

The most thanks, as always, to Tina, Nate, and Will who shared 'the seething and colourful life'.

'why do you dress me/ In borrowed robes?' (*Macbeth* I, iii, 108–09)

'I was quite sure that *Hamlet* had only one possible interpretation, and that one universally obvious.' (Laura Bohannan, 'Shakespeare in the Bush')

'Every nation, every race, has not only its own creative, but its own critical turn of mind; and is even more oblivious of the shortcomings and limitations of its critical habits than of those of its creative genius.' (T.S. Eliot, 'Tradition and the Individual Talent')

Preface

The globalization of literature is not a new phenomenon, but its pace has surely quickened with modern technological advances in transportation and communication. Cultural 'commodities' like Shakespeare are sometimes considered socioeconomic export products from an imperialist West bent on the explicit or implicit exploitation, depreciation, and/or assimilation of unique local cultures. On the other hand, various peoples – the Han Chinese, for instance – have happily interpreted, shaped, and adapted Shakespeare to their own needs and desires, appropriated and expropriated the Bard to serve their own particular ends. Shakespeare in the Chinas, as we shall see, is very much intertwined with Chinese politics, traditions, and societies.

Even today many People's Republic Shakespeare scholars, translators, and theatre people still begin with ideological assumptions and dated models, and tailor their analyses or productions to these assumptions and models. But now there is an important distinction to be made between older generation Shakespeareans, who remember campaigns against intellectuals and the Cultural Revolution and are understandably cautious, and the younger generation with a freer and more global viewpoint. The PRC is changing rapidly in many areas – even when it comes to Shakespeare. Chinese theatre festivals and international conferences, together with scholars and directors travelling abroad, have brought foreign approaches and new ideas to recent Chinese Shakespeare activity. In addition, more and more young Chinese Shakespeareans study in the West or with foreign Shakespeare 'experts' at home, and have access to recent scholarship and accounts of productions via imported books, journals, and, of course, the Internet.

And Shakespeare is popular beyond the mainland. As might be expected, the Bard arrived in Hong Kong with the colonizers, at first for their own cultural security and then to edify the 'barbarians'. Shakespeare soon became part of the island's school curriculum. With Hong Kong now reunited with the mainland, the issue of Shakespeare involves Sino-cultural pride, and repressed, suppressed, and expressed anti-colonial sentiments. But increasingly Hong Kong theatre companies are staging Shakespeare with ever more professionalism, and mostly in Cantonese. In Taiwan, Shakespeareans exhibit a more general, global interest in the Bard, and are sometimes daring in their recent stage productions. Scholars and critics participate in the current international conversations, and theatre people feel free to use Shakespeare as a jumping-off point for exploring current social issues. In short, Chinese Shakespeare is various and interesting.

* * *

My curiosity about Shakespeare in the Chinas began when Skidmore College granted me a sabbatical leave for the academic year 1987–88, a year I spent with my family in Qufu (Confucius' 'home town'), Shandong Province. This curiosity was prompted by a graduate course I taught to two wonderful students, Yi Yong and Ju Yumei, at Qufu Teachers University. Some of my fondest memories of this time include discussing Shakespeare weekly over green tea, and walking to town in a light December snow to see Sergei Youtkevich's version of *Othello* at a local theatre – a 1955 Russian film of a seventeenth-century English play dubbed in Mandarin! (I was impressed that Shakespeare was showing at one of only two theatres in the small provincial town of Qufu, and to a full house.)

This book is aimed specifically at Shakespeareans interested in learning about the Bard's history and reception in China in the twentieth century. I envision mostly a Western readership, but I trust that even Chinese Shakespeare scholars and theatre people might learn new things from my study. Much of the previous scholarship I build on is not readily available in the West, and some has not been translated before. When appropriate I use previously published translations, including ones that I have had a hand in.

The task of rendering Chinese words and names has presented real challenges throughout. Most are spelled in standard *pinyin* or the Wade–Giles style of romanization, but some few are not. I kept the authors' names mostly as they appear in their publications (but not in Chinese characters), and use the *pinyin* system for words. I strove always for clarity.

CHAPTER ONE

The Early History of Shakespeare in China

'What light through yonder window breaks?' (*Romeo and Juliet* II, ii, 1–2)

Confucius asks, at the beginning of *The Analects* [*Lun yu*], 'Is it not a joy to have friends come from afar?'[1] And China has warmly welcomed her foreign friend Shakespeare for much of the twentieth century and into the new millennium. The playwright guest, however, born in the forty-third year of Emperor Jiajing's Ming Dynasty reign, apparently knew little about the country that has recently adopted him enthusiastically. Shakespeare did know that China produced fine porcelain, the expensive and newly fashionable English import, as he notes in *Measure for Measure*: 'they are not china dishes, but very good dishes' (II, i, 94).[2] He is also aware of the fearsome Mongolian Emperor Kubla Khan, who ruled in the Yuan Dynasty. It was a monumental task, as Benedick affirms, to 'fetch . . . a hair off the Great Cham's beard' (*Much Ado About*

---

[1] Trans. D.C. Lau, Harmondsworth: Penguin Books, 1979: 59. Note that full bibliographic references are given at first mention; subsequent references appear in short title or abbreviated form in parentheses in the text.
[2] All Shakespeare quotations noted in the text are from *The Riverside Shakespeare*, 2nd edn, textual eds. G. Blakemore Evans and J.J.M. Tobin, Boston: Houghton Mifflin, 1997.

Nothing, II, i, 268–69). The playwright seems to use 'Cataian' to mean 'Chinese' (the word derived from *Cathay* for 'China'), employing it as a term of abuse, suggesting 'rogue', 'scoundrel', 'cheater', or 'liar' (see OED). This can be observed in *The Merry Wives of Windsor* when Page so labels Falstaff: 'I will not believe such a Cataian, though the priest o' th' town commend him for a true man' (II, i, 144–46). Sir Toby, too, in *Twelfth Night*, uses the word to describe Olivia in one of his explosive outbursts: 'My lady's a Cataian' (II, iii, 75).[3] But these very few references are all one finds concerning China or Chinese in Shakespeare's work.

Shakespeare might have read about China in, for example, Montaigne's *essais* 'Of Coaches' or 'Of Experience'. In the former, the Frenchman acknowledges China as the inventor of artillery and printing a thousand years before the Europeans, and in the latter he writes, 'In China the policy, arts and government of which kingdome, having neither knowledge or commerce with ours; exceed our examples in divers parts of excellency; and whose Histories teach me, how much more ample and divers the World is, than eyther we or our forefathers could ever enter into.'[4] The playwright/poet may also have caught wind of Queen Elizabeth's and King James's several unsuccessful attempts to instigate trade with the Middle Kingdom. In any case, my subject is not Shakespeare's knowledge of China or his view of the Chinese, but rather China's knowledge of Shakespeare – specifically in this chapter, the early history of the Bard and the Dragon to late 1949, the year of the communist victory on the mainland. After a brief introductory section, I consider three main subjects: early translations, productions, and commentary.

---

[3] The Oxford editors spell the word 'Cathayan' in their edition, and cite Gustav Ungerer's contention that it does not refer to Chinese at all, but is rather Sir Toby's slur for 'Catharan', the medieval Latin for *pure*. See *Twelfth Night*, eds Roger Warren and Stanley Wells, Oxford: Oxford University Press, 1994: 127, n.71.

[4] *The Essayes of Montaigne*, trans. John Florio, New York: The Modern Library, 1900: 820, 969.

* * *

Shakespeare arrived in the Middle Kingdom long after the Tang Priest, Monkey, Friar Sand, and Piggy took their 'journey to the West', as narrated in the famous sixteenth-century Chinese epic of that name, to bring back to China the Buddhist sutras, those other sacred texts. The first discovered reference to Shakespeare is contained in a book of British history translated and published in 1856. Between 1877 and 1879 Guo Songtao (1818–91), the Qing minister in England, notes the Bard thrice in his diary. He includes mention of a Henry Irving *Hamlet* seen at London's Lyceum Theatre on January 18, 1879. With only a few other passing references to Shakespeare by educated Chinese and in books written, translated, or edited by Christian missionaries in China, the poet/playwright was virtually unknown to the Chinese before the turning of the twentieth century.

During this century past, China, to be sure, has fluctuated between xenophobic isolationism and openness to other cultures and ideas. The waning and fall of the Qing Dynasty and events leading up to the democratic revolution of 1911 brought with them calls by intellectuals for an end to traditional feudalistic ways and an engagement with Western art, thought, and science. In 1907 Lu Xun, considered by many the father of modern Chinese literature, mentions Shakespeare in passing, in three essays written when he was a student in Japan. In 'The History of Science' Lu insists, 'a society needs . . . not only Newton but also Shakespeare [because] a writer like Shakespeare can make people have a sound and perfect human nature [that is, become more human].'[5] In 'On Cultural Bias', and using the crowd reactions to Antony's and Brutus' forum speeches as illustrations, he makes the Nietzschean point that the masses should never be trusted with the truth, and that world peace depends on political supermen (a position he was

---

[5] Quoted in Zhang Xiaoyang, *Shakespeare in China: A Comparative Study of Two Traditions and Cultures*, Newark: University of Delaware Press, 1996: 101–02.

later to revise). Lastly, in 'On the Function of Poetry', Lu hopes 'for the emergence of a Shakespeare-like Chinese writer to give voice to China's national spirit'.[6]

Early Translations

In *A Midsummer Night's Dream*, Tom Snout and Peter Quince, shocked and frightened by Bottom's bizarre transformation, exclaim: 'O Bottom, thou art changed! . . . Bless thee, Bottom, bless thee! Thou art translated' (III, i, 114; 118–19). Shakespeare came to China similarly transmogrified and through the 'back door'. At the beginning, in 1903, he was introduced by way of Charles and Mary Lamb's *Tales From Shakespeare*. Ten of these children's stories were anonymously rendered into *wenyan wen*-style classical Chinese in a volume whose title translates *Strange Tales From Abroad* [*Xiewai qitan*]. The author's 'Preface' had this to say about Shakespeare:

> He was a world-renowned actor, an accomplished poet, an extraordinarily popular playwright, and is considered a literary giant in England. His works have been translated into French, German, Russian, and Italian, and are read by almost everyone. Our own contemporary literati who specialize in writing verse and fiction have also joined the chorus in his praise *without even having had the opportunity to read his work* [italics mine!]. To remedy this unfortunate situation, I have undertaken this translation with the hope that it will add color and splendor to the world of fiction (quoted in Meng, *Survey*: 6).

The unnamed translator arranged the Lambs' *Tales* as traditional Chinese classical fiction (*zhanghui xiaoshuo*), in chapters with couplet head notes anticipating the plots. Thus, *The Two Gentlemen of*

---

[6] Quoted in Meng Xianqiang, *A Historical Survey of Shakespeare in China*, trans. Mason Y.H. Wang and Murray J. Levith, Changchun: Shakespeare Research Centre of Northeast Normal University, 1996: 4.

Verona becomes 'Proteus Betrays His Good Friend For the Sake of Gratifying His Lust', *The Merchant of Venice* becomes 'Antonio Borrows Money by Agreeing to Have His Flesh Cut [If He Defaults]', 'Olivia Makes a Mistake in Love With the Twin Sister of Sebastian', 'Hamlet Takes Revenge by Slaying His Uncle', and so on. With the exception of *Hamlet* and two romances, all the translations were of comedies.[7]

One year later, a comprehensive version of *Tales From Shakespeare* appeared with the title *The Mystery Fiction of the English Poet*. This time the author acknowledged his work. Lin Shu (also known as Lin Qinnan), helped by Wei Chunshu (Wei Yi), rendered the play stories, again setting them down in classical Chinese.[8] Incredibly, Lin didn't know English, and so Wei summarized the plots for him before he wrote them out. These so-called 'translations' happened accidentally according to Lin's account: 'When free one night, Mr. Wei picked up some Shakespeare by chance; I started scribbling away by the night lamp. Twenty days later we have a book of Shakespeare's poetic tales.'[9] Just as did the anonymous author, Lin gave his narratives new titles – for example, *Fated Love (Zhuqing)* for *Romeo and Juliet*, *Flesh Bond (Rouquan)* for *The Merchant of Venice*, and *A Ghost's Summons (Guizhao)* for *Hamlet*. This practice of changing Shakespeare's traditional play titles subsequently became typical for many Chinese translators. Lin's 'Preface' praises Shakespeare's poetry, comparing it to the great Tang Dynasty poet Du Fu (712–70), but, as a good Confucian and perhaps to anticipate criticism for choosing Shakespeare to translate in the first place, he also castigates the playwright for his non-scientific 'superstition'.

---

[7] The others were *The Comedy of Errors*, *The Taming of the Shrew*, *All's Well That Ends Well*, *Measure for Measure*, *Cymbeline*, and *The Winter's Tale*.

[8] A noted scholar who taught at various prestigious universities, Lin Shu (1852–1924) rendered almost two hundred works of Western literature into classical Chinese.

[9] Quoted in Faye Chunfang Fei, *Chinese Theories of Theatre and Performance from Confucius to the Present*, Ann Arbor: University of Michigan Press, 1999: 115–16.

Lin writes of Shakespeare that 'he often conjures up images of gods, fairies, ghosts, and demons. If the Westerners are so civilized, then maybe these works mentioned should be banned and burned so as not to interfere with scientific knowledge' (quoted in Fei, *Theories*: 114–15).[10] Strange sentiments for a translator! Lin rendered one of the Lambs' stories each day, and his versions are still regarded as excellent models of elegant Chinese prose. The Lambs, of course, included only twenty plays in their *Tales*, and none of the histories. After a few more years, however, Lin, this time with Chen Jialin, offered five other play stories, among them *Richard II*, and *Henry IV, Parts 1 and 2*. Lin also published the three parts of *Henry VI* in 1916, and *Henry V* was printed posthumously in 1924.[11] But even then China's encounter with Shakespeare's plots was still obviously incomplete.

It should be noted further that Lin's 'refinements' of the Lambs' already streamlined tales also included significant departures, as did some of the Lambs' stories, from Shakespeare's original plots. In Lin's *Hamlet*, for instance, the prince is *married* to Ophelia, blames himself for killing his father-in-law Polonius, composes the entire *Gonzago* play, etc. The tale also has a decided Confucian flavour, emphasizing the important relationships between king and subject, parent and child, brother and brother, and husband and wife.[12]

* * *

[10] There was at this time a movement that advocated modern science as a way for 'backward' China to catch up with the West.

[11] Chang Chen-Hsien writes that after seeing Gounod's *Romeo and Juliet* in 1910 Lin also translated the balcony scene into a 'rhymed ballad' ('Shakespeare in China', *Shakespeare Survey 6*, ed. Allardyce Nicoll, Cambridge: Cambridge University Press, 1953: 114). The modern vernacular version of the Lambs' *Tales* was translated by Xiao Qian and published in 1956.

[12] For these observations, I am indebted to Ching-Hsi Perng's lecture, 'Chinese *Hamlets*: A Centenary Review', delivered September 2000, at De Monfort University, Leicester, UK.

In 1917 Hu Shi and the New Culture Movement advocated the modern spoken vernacular rather than formal, classical Chinese as an acceptable medium for serious literature and scholarship. The influential May Fourth Movement, formed two years later, endorsed this call, and, spurred on by it, interest not only in modern written Chinese but also in foreign literature, including Western drama, increased enormously. However, it was not until 1922 that a full play text by Shakespeare was translated into standard spoken Chinese and published in book form.[13] The celebrated playwright Tian Han's translation of *Hamlet* [*Hamengleite*], the first three scenes of which were published in the journal *Young China* in 1921, was this important milestone.[14] Tian had read Shakespeare with interest and excitement during his student days in Japan, and he planned to translate nine more plays into vernacular Chinese, but after *Hamlet* only *Romeo and Juliet* was forthcoming (1924). However, Tian's work inspired others in the later twenties, and various translators published versions of *The Taming of the Shrew*, *The Merchant of Venice*, *Julius Caesar*, *As You Like It*, *The Merry Wives of Windsor*, another *Hamlet* and another *Romeo and Juliet*.

But the big Shakespeare translation projects were yet to come. In 1924 the United States Congress forgave $12.5 million of the Boxer indemnity (the huge sum the Qing government agreed to pay the victorious foreign powers after the suppression of the Boxer Rebellion) on the condition that this money be spent to

---

[13] Ho Hsiang-Lin notes that the first translation from a Shakespeare text into classical Chinese was Bao Tianxiao's *The Merchant of Venice* in 1904 ('Shakespeare in China', *The Comparatist* 13 [1989]: 11).

[14] During the Cultural Revolution Tian Han was denounced as a 'bourgeoise revisionist', imprisoned and tortured. See the *People's Daily* article of March 2, 1971, reprinted in Kai-yu Hsu, *The Chinese Literary Scene: A Writer's Visit to the People's Republic*, New York: Vintage, 1975: 43–50. Ironically, Tian is author of the words to the People's Republic of China's national anthem.

advance Chinese education and culture.[15] The duly formed Translation Division of the China Educational and Cultural Foundation, headed by Hu Shi, selected Harvard-educated Professor Liang Shiqiu, then Chair of the English Department of the National Shandong University in Qingdao, to be part of a committee of five to attempt a translation of Shakespeare's complete works into Chinese.[16] The project was to begin in 1930 and was meant to take five to ten years to complete (Zhang, *Shakespeare*: 105–06). As an experiment, some of the initial translations were to be in poetry and some in prose, in order to determine the best way to proceed.[17] However, because of financial and bureaucratic difficulties, as well as the death of one of its scholars (Xu Zhimo) in a plane crash, the committee never met and disbanded before any work could be accomplished. Undaunted, Professor Liang resolved to attempt alone the formidable task of translating all of Shakespeare. In 1936 he published his first translations: *As You Like It*, *Twelfth Night*, *The Merchant of Venice*, *Hamlet*, and *Macbeth*. Though slowed by the war years, he continued to work, next publishing translations of *A Midsummer Night's Dream* and the two parts of *Henry IV*. After fleeing to Taiwan with the Nationalists in 1949, he pressed on and completed his edition there, a labour of more than thirty years. Published in Taiwan in 1967–68, it is based on W.J. Craig's 1930 Oxford University Press edition. Liang's forty-volume *Shakespeare* (thirty-seven of the plays and three of the poems) contains about three million Chinese characters, and is a generously annotated prose version. Professor Liang explained that his rationale for choosing prose for his trans-

---

[15] In the 1901 Boxer Protocol, which followed suppression of the Boxer Rebellion, the Qing government agreed to pay the victorious foreign powers a large indemnity. See Jonathan Spence, *The Search For Modern China*, New York: Norton, 1990: 384, 790.

[16] The other committee members were Wen Yiduo, Zhen Dongbo, Xu Zhimo, and Ye Gongchao.

[17] Rudolph J. Chu, 'Shakespeare in China: Translations and Translators', *Tamkang Review* 1:2 (October 1970): 175.

lations was because there is no 'blank verse' form in Chinese poetry. Furthermore, he argued, when plays are performed the actors do not recite or chant the verse; that is, the poetry sounds like prose on the stage.

Liang's *Shakespeare* is not universally admired. Cao Weifeng, for example, criticized these translations early on; he saw them as 'merely a narration of the stories word by word without giving any attention to the marvelous artistic accomplishment of the original texts' (quoted in Meng, *Survey*: 12). But perhaps there was some competitive jealousy in this criticism, for Cao had begun his own translation of the complete works in 1930. He ultimately finished only fifteen plays, most of them comedies, eleven of which were published between 1942 and 1944 with the anticipatory title *The Complete Works of Shakespeare* (Meng, *Survey*: 24).[18]

But a more serious critic of Liang, and not specifically for his Shakespeare, was Mao Zedong himself. He attacked the professor on ideological grounds for his belief that literature often contains universal themes. Mao writes, 'People like Liang Shi-ch'iu [Liang Shiqiu] . . . may talk about art and literature as transcending the classes, but in fact they all uphold bourgeois art and literature in opposition to proletarian art and literature'.[19] In a vitriolic footnote, Mao identifies Liang as 'a counter-revolutionary member of the National Socialist Party, who propagated American reactionary bourgeoisie literary theory and criticized revolutionary literature'. To be sure, in a 1926 essay, Liang had argued that all great literature reflects the universality of human nature, and he goes on to suggest, in 'Literature and Revolution', published two years later, that literature has no class bias:

What the writer represents is the common human character. . . .
He cannot have any special responsibility toward the masses and

---

[18] Cao's translations were decidedly literary versions, not written for the stage.

[19] Mao Tse-Tung [Zedong], 'Talks at the Yenan Forum on Art and Literature', *Selected Works 4 (1941–1945)*, New York: International Publishers, 1956: 71.

certainly no capacity for altering human life; . . . the masses have no literature and therefore literature is not for the masses. . . . Proletarian literature or literature for the masses cannot be established, because literature fundamentally depends upon human personality and does not recognize any class distinction.[20]

By 1934 Lu Xun ridiculed Liang and his colleagues, who formed what was known as the Crescent Moon faction, for something else. He taunted them for not having produced a complete Shakespeare in the Chinese language, especially considering that some in the group knew English and had studied in England (Meng, *Survey*: 21). Lu himself, as we have mentioned, had been a student in Japan, and he called attention to the many world masterpieces available in Japanese translation. Tsubouchi Shoyo, for example, had published his translation of Shakespeare's complete plays and sonnets in 1928.[21] Why then was there no complete Shakespeare in Chinese? To accomplish one would be a patriotic act. Not only were Professor Liang and Cao Weifeng already at work on such a project, but soon thereafter an obscure editor in Shanghai also took up the challenge.

Zhu Shenghao (1911–44) is arguably the most celebrated Chinese translator of Shakespeare. He studied both Chinese and English literature at Zhejiang University in Hangzhou, and following graduation was employed by the Shanghai World Book Company. At age twenty-four, after prompting from his supervisor and older brother, he set himself a goal to translate all of

---

[20] Quoted in Amitendranath Tagore, *Literary Debates in Modern China, 1918–1937*, Tokyo: The Centre for Eastern Asian Cultural Studies, 1967: 108–09. See Lu Xun's answer to Liang's first essay: 'Literature and Sweat', *Lu Hsun: Writing for the Revolution*, San Francisco: Red Sun Publishers, 1976: 27–28.

[21] James R. Brandon, 'Some Shakespeare(s) in Some Asia(s)', *Asian Studies Review* 20:3 (April 1997): 6.

Shakespeare, and almost succeeded despite war and a fatal illness (Meng, *Survey*: 21). Zhu writes:

In the spring of 1935, encouraged by my colleague Zhan Wenhu, I began an attempt to translate the complete works. Unfortunately, the war broke out the following year, and all my editions, critical works, and textual studies collected over a long period, more than two hundred volumes, were destroyed. What I was able to carry away in haste were the one-volume Oxford Shakespeare and a few of my draft translations. I led a vagabond's life for many years, driven from place to place and struggling to survive, with little time to work on the translation project. As the world situation became more desperate in the spring of 1942, I decided to lock myself up at home and concentrate solely on my project. Despite poverty and illness I continued to work at my desk, and after ten years have finally completed the task. Ten years to complete the difficult task of translating Shakespeare cannot be regarded as overly long, but I have expended all my energy and strength on it.[22]

Zhu, in fact, did not actually finish translating all of the plays; he completed thirty-one and part of another by the time of his death from tuberculosis at age thirty-three. Song Qingru, his widow, reported that his deathbed words were: 'Had I known I would not rise again after this illness, I would have exerted all my efforts to complete the translation' (quoted in Meng, *Survey*: 23). In 1947 Zhu's version of twenty-seven plays was published together with a 'Preface', written eight months before he died, meant to introduce his completed edition; and in 1954 all of Zhu's finished work saw print. Zhu began with a translation of *The Tempest*, completed in 1936, and his early plan was to translate everything in only two years! In the first year alone, he completed almost eight plays (Chu, 'Shakespeare': 171). His translation principles are as follows:

I do my best for conserving the flavor and features of the style

---

[22] 'Translator's Preface', *Complete Works of Shakespeare* [*Shashibiya quanji*], 11 vols. Beijing: People's Publishing House, 1978: 2–3.

of the original. In case I failed to reach this goal, I would try to communicate the ideas . . . clearly and faithfully in an elegant and comprehensible Chinese. I considered it indecent to translate word for word without expressing the ingenuity and vigor of the original.

Whenever I felt unable to render an English sentence into Chinese adequately, I would work a long time on it, and strive to reveal the English poet's ideas clearly, risking a completely different rearrangement of the words of the original sentence. Every time I finished translating a paragraph, I used to read it carefully as [if I were] the first reader . . . [to see] if there were any ambiguities, and at the same time I would consider myself an actor for examining if the tone of the version was harmonical [*sic*] and the rhythm was agreeable. If, for example, a word or a sentence were not used with good taste, I would meditate even for some days trying hard to find the right word (quoted in Chu, 'Shakespeare': 170).

Zhu's dedicated work ultimately provided the basis for a complete Chinese Shakespeare, with the missing material translated by Yu Erchang, Zhu's university classmate and later professor at National Taiwan University, and published in Taiwan in 1966. On the mainland, Zhu's project was edited by Wu Xinghua, Fang Ping, and Fang Chung, completed by various scholars, and published in 1978.[23] Zhu's translations, popular to this day, are considered by many to be the very best due to their fluency and sensitivity to Shakespeare's nuances of diction and word play. His versions of the tragedies are especially celebrated (Chu, 'Shakespeare': 174). However, Zhu's *Shakespeare*, though universally acknowledged as a monumental achievement, is not

---

[23] The translators were Fang Ping (*Henry V*), Zhang Yi (*1–3 Henry VI*), Fang Chung (*Richard III*), Yang Zhouhan (*Henry VIII*), Zhang Guruo ('Venus and Adonis'), Yang Deyu ('The Rape of Lucrece'), Liang Zongdai ('The Sonnets'), and Huang Yushi ('The Phoenix and the Turtle' and 'A Lover's Complaint').

praised unconditionally by everyone. Some scholars complain because it is rendered in prose rather than poetry, and others cite various inaccuracies.[24] Yang Zhouhan, for one, sees Zhu's translation of *King Lear* as lacking when compared, say, with Sun Dayu's rendering of the same tragedy: 'Sun Dayu's translation is far superior to that by Zhu Shenghao because the former demonstrates a profounder understanding of the play. The difference in quality is due, in large measure, to this understanding but also to the superior command of the Chinese language'.[25]

Sun Dayu based his translation on the 1880 H. H. Furness *King Lear* variorum edition, and completed his *Lear* in 1941. Ultimately published in 1948, it is considered 'the first full-text [poetry] version of Shakespeare in Chinese'.[26] Sun's 'Preface' discusses the almost insurmountable difficulty of translating Shakespeare into vernacular Chinese verse due to the vast differences between the English and Chinese languages.[27] Sun states that accomplishing a 'perfect translation' would indeed be a 'miracle'. An instance of the problem is the complexity of the word 'be', for example in Hamlet's 'To be, or not to be' soliloquy; it cannot be rendered adequately in Chinese. Similarly, in *King Lear* there is no single word to capture the multiple meanings of 'nothing'. Further, rendering the word 'nature' as *xiao* for a Chinese may call up Confucian notions of filial piety rather than Shakespeare's intended denotative and connotative meanings (see Yang, '*Lear*': 263). Criticizing previous

---

[24] See He Xianglin, 'Some Comments on Zhu Shenghao's Translation of Shakespeare's Plays', *Essays on Shakespeare*, ed. He Xianglin, Xian: Shaanxi People's Publishing House, 1982: 294–314; and, Bian Zhilin, 'On Translating *Hamlet* into Chinese and on the Chinese Dubbing of the Film Version', *Shakespeare Studies (China)* 1 (1983): 6–25; noted in He Qixin, 'On Translating Shakespeare into Chinese', M.A. thesis: University of Akron, 1984: 10.

[25] '*King Lear* Metamorphosed', *Comparative Literature* 39 (1987): 263.

[26] *Beijing Review* 28: 1 (7 January 1985): 45.

[27] 'Preface' to *Shakespeare Criticism in China*, ed. Meng Xianqiang, Changchun: Jilin Education Press, 1991: 111–20.

but unnamed translators not fluent in English, and who clearly rely on dictionaries and Japanese versions of Shakespeare's plays, Sun takes to task particularly those who change Shakespeare's poetry into prose. Thus, Sun invents for his *King Lear* a Chinese equivalent for Shakespeare's blank verse, *yinzu* or 'sound unit', based upon phoneme groupings. His idea is that because vernacular Chinese words are often composed of two or three characters (and rarely four), which may be seen as akin to syllables, something approximating a five beat blank verse line can be suggested. Sun's desire is that his *King Lear* recreates the 'spirit' of the original play, which he feels is what Schlegal and Tieck accomplished with their famous German version.

Cao Yu (d. 1996), perhaps China's most celebrated modern dramatist and one whose own plays show Shakespeare's influence, translated a free verse *Romeo and Juliet* [*Roumiou yu Youliye*] in the early forties,[28] and Liang Zongdai rendered thirty of the sonnets in 1944. Prior to 1949, the plays especially favoured by translators were *Hamlet, Romeo and Juliet, Julius Caesar*, and *The Merchant of Venice*, each available in five different versions, and in general the tragedies received the most attention. In all thirty-one Shakespeare plays appeared in Chinese by mid-century. Understandably, given the foreignness of English history, six of the chronicle plays were rendered last. Indeed, the first full-text publication of a history play had to wait for Zhu Shenghao in 1947.

Early Productions

Adaptations from the Lambs found their way onto the Chinese stage beginning in 1913.[29] They were usually performed in the

---

[28] Cao Yu presented the 1960 edition of this translation to the Shakespeare Institute, Stratford-upon-Avon, in 1980.

[29] There was, however, a 1902 staging of *The Merchant of Venice* in English, presumably an original text version, at St. John's College, Shanghai, and Rudolph Chu notes that 'before Shakespeare's dramas were

mubiaozhi style, characterized by improvisational performance around the given plot line, somewhat in the manner of the Italian *commedia dell'arte*. As was traditional in the Chinese theatre as well as in Shakespeare's own, the actors were all male.[30] *The Merchant of Venice* was the first to be staged, and early productions of the comedy were variously titled *A Pound of Flesh* [*Yibang rou*], *Securing a Loan by Pledging Flesh-Cutting* [*Jiejai gerou*], and *The Woman Attorney* [*Nu lushi*], indicating the play's interpretive slant. A newspaper advertisement for this last production reports that *The Woman Attorney* is 'one of Shakespeare's famous plays. It involves cutting off a piece of one's own flesh [*sic*] to borrow money while the heroine, though a woman, still becomes a lawyer. Excellent literary style; a wonderful story full of fun' (Li, 'Bard': 55). Heroines in disguise and unscrupulous usurers were familiar figures in many Chinese folk tales, but Western religious conflicts and prejudices obviously were not of much interest. Shakespeare's *Merchant* also exerted some general influence on the Chinese stage of the time, and actor Wang Youyou was noted for his *Merchant* performance.

Mounted in 1914 was an *Othello* [*Wosailuo*] culled from the Lambs, with Chinese character names substituted for Shakespeare's originals (which became a common Chinese practice), and *The Taming of the Shrew* [*Xunhanji*], *Romeo and Juliet* [*Zhuqing*], and others followed. In these early years as many as twenty Shakespeare plays were performed, largely in the modern style known as *wenmingxi*. This 'civilized drama' was another name for the 'new drama' [*xinju*] and later so-called 'spoken (or talk) drama' [*huaju*] introduced to the Chinese theatre by students who had studied abroad and/or had been exposed to foreign dramatic forms, techniques, and styles. Such drama indicated a departure

---

received by the Chinese literary public, other playwrights [Ibsen, Moliere, etc.] had already been very popular in China' ('Shakespeare': 157).
[30] Li Ruru, 'The Bard in the Middle Kingdom', *Asian Theatre Journal* 12:1 (Spring 1995): 51–2.

from the received tradition, which was often associated with China's humiliations of the too recent past, and signalled the emergence of a vibrant new patriotic and nationalistic spirit. Typically the modern style further simplified even the Lambs' rather simple plot outlines, and again gave Shakespeare's plays new names (such as, *Twin Brother and Sister* for *Twelfth Night*, *The Unhappy Couple Becomes Happily Married* for *Much Ado About Nothing*, *The Physician's Daughter* for *All's Well That Ends Well*, *Gratitude and Resentment Incurred By a Ring* for *Cymbeline*, and *Hating Gold* for *Timon of Athens*).

In 1915 a remarkable event occurred, reminiscent of the *Richard II* propaganda production supporting the Essex Rebellion.[31] When the powerful warlord Yuan Shikai (1859–1916) declared himself emperor, an adaptation of *Hamlet* was offered in Shanghai with a title that translates *Usurping the Throne and Stealing a Sister-in-Law* [*Cuanwei daosao*] – to make the opposition's political point. In the same year, another *Hamlet*, with the title *Arch Usurper of the State* [*Qieguo zei*], was advertised, using a clever mixture of poetry and prose:

> A subject, he steals the throne and the nation, and commits adultery with the queen;
> A brother, he steals his sister-in-law and [his brother's] regime.
> The murder of his father must be avenged, especially when the mother is married with the murderer! [The prince] cannot choose but pretend madness [to probe] his mother. In the end, nobody escapes death. How horribly tragic is this tragedy?[32]

---

[31] We recall that the Earl of Essex, Robert Devereux, planned a *coup d'etat* to be supported with a 1601 staging of *Richard II* by Shakespeare's company, the Lord Chamberlain's Men. Shakespeare's play, to be sure, includes the deposition of the monarch.

[32] I am indebted to Ching-Hsi Perng for this translation. The advertisement is reprinted in Cao Shujun and Sun Fuliang, *Shashibiya zai Zhongguo wutaishang* [*Shakespeare on the Chinese Stage*], Harbin: Harbin chubanshe, 1989: 81.

Macbeth was also produced, apparently with the same title, *Arch Usurper of the State*.[33] During these *Macbeth* performances, the actor Gu Wuwei, in various asides, ad-libbed sarcastic insults about the self-proclaimed emperor, and sympathetic audiences cheered these slights. The outraged Yuan had Gu arrested, imprisoned, and summarily sentenced to death without trial, but the would-be monarch soon fell from power and died himself before Gu's execution could be carried out.

Another more conventional version of *Macbeth*, titled *Curses of the Witches*, was also mounted during this same early period, and a number of other Shakespeare plays were also staged.[34] All were clearly adapted from the Lambs' *Tales*.

In the 1920s, actresses began playing the female roles in 'new' drama productions. Also at this time, the Amateur Performance Movement [*Aimeiju yundong*] encouraged the formation of many non-professional theatre groups, and there were numerous school productions of Shakespeare. In 1924, for example, the New Learning College [*Xinxue shuyuan*] put on *The Merchant of Venice* in English, and a few years later the Zhongxi Girls' School mounted an *As You Like It* (Meng, *Survey*: 17). However, it was not until the 1930s that the first productions true to a Shakespeare text occurred on the Chinese stage. At the start of the decade, the Drama League of Shanghai performed Gu Zhongyi's translation of *The Merchant of Venice* in eight scenes, and this production is considered the first original-text performance of Shakespeare in China (*Beijing Review*: 45). It featured sixteenth- and seventeenth-century period costumes and scenery suggested by Renaissance Italian paintings. Another important early staging of an actual play text was Tian Han's version of *Romeo and Juliet*, offered by a Shanghai amateur troupe in 1937, but with professional actors in the major roles[35]. A

---

[33] See discussion of this *Hamlet* and *Macbeth* in Li, 'Bard': 52, 77–78, n.8.
[34] See list in Ibid.: 52–53.
[35] See, Yu Weijie, *The Dramatic Touch of Difference: Theatre Own and Foreign*, eds Erika Fischer–Lichte, Josephine Riley and Michael Gissenwehrer, Tubinger: Gunter Narr, 1990: 161–67.

Stanislavsky-inspired production, it reportedly featured a realistic 'vault scene' and prop swords so sharp that actors were injured during rehearsals and performances. Critics found the translation stilted and not well suited to the stage.[36] However, this *Romeo and Juliet* and the debate it elicited, according to Li Ruru, was important because it served to initiate 'a link between translation, performance, and criticism in the history of the "Shakespeare enterprise" in China' (Li, 'Bard': 59).[37]

Another 1937 production was *The Merchant of Venice*, mounted in Nanjing at The National Academy for Theatrical Performance, just before China entered World War II. Translator Liang Shiqiu attended a performance and notes his response:

> Some parts of my version were changed for the purpose of accommodating them to the conditions of the stage. . . . Moreover, some sentences were also adapted according to the familiar language. This is an evidence that my version was still too formal. That is to say, the sentences were not easy and fluent enough. This presentation on stage was the best critic of my work (quoted in Chu, 'Shakespeare': 164).

Accompanying this *Merchant* production was a seminar on Shakespeare's comedy, a newspaper supplement about the play, and a volume of eight essays published by the National Academy.

The year 1938 saw Liang's version of *Othello* produced, and his *Hamlet*, after long months of preparation and rehearsal, was on the stage in 1942 in wartime Chongqing [Chung-king]. According to director Jiao Junjin, Shakespeare's *Hamlet* contained important contemporary lessons for the Chinese in their fight against Japanese aggression: 'the conclusion we can draw from the tra-

---

[36] Chang Chen-Hsien, 'Shakespeare in China', M.A. thesis: University of Birmingham, 1951: 8–9.

[37] Li also notes an overlooked *Romeo and Juliet* in the *jingju* (Beijing Opera) style earlier in the decade.

gedy of Hamlet is that victory in our Anti-Japanese war will depend on the joint action taken by the people all over the country. . . . This is the significance underlying our introduction of *Hamlet* to Chinese audiences' (quoted in Li, 'Bard': 61). However, these same audiences reportedly found the foreignness of Jiao's production difficult to comprehend (Chang, 'Shakespeare' [thesis]: 3). For example, according to traditional Chinese dramatic conventions, heroes are not rude to their mothers and don't die in the end. Similarly, an obedient daughter in a play is not 'punished' by going mad and committing suicide.

Jiao's *Hamlet* prompted a *New York Times* page one review by theatre critic Brooks Atkinson. He writes, 'Sincere and painstaking though this "Hamlet" may be, it is not yet ready for Broadway'.[38] Atkinson faintly praised the costumes and stage designer's 'good taste', but the reviewer, on the other hand, found the music accompanying the production – a Handel 'Largo' and Beethoven's 'Minuet in G' – a bit odd for Shakespeare's *Hamlet*. Even more remarkable and 'disconcerting' to the critic were the actors' artificial noses! Atkinson continues, 'the Kuo-Tsi [Theatre] actors have built up a series of proboscises fearful to behold. The king has a monstrous, pendulous nose that would serve valiantly in a burlesque show; Polonius has a pointed nose and sharply flaring mustache of the Hohenzollern type; Hamlet cuts his way through with a nose fashioned like a plowshare.' It promised to be a very late night for the critic, and he admits leaving the theatre before the play's end. Cao Yu's version of *Romeo and Juliet* was staged more successfully during the war years, with popular film stars playing the leads. A wartime production of *Macbeth* also received some praise.

Commentary

Dong Run's series of four articles, published in 1917 and 1918, are considered by many scholars to be the first notable Chinese

---

[38] 'The Play', *New York Times*, 18 December 1942: 1, 38.

Shakespeare 'studies'. In an essay in the *Pacific* (July 1917), Dong suggests that his observations about the playwright might help people in conversation with English speakers, since Shakespeare is a subject that inevitability arises in such exchanges.[39] Dong notes Lin Shu's 'translations' from the Lambs', and reviews details of Shakespeare's life. He considers Shakespeare 'liberal' because he marries an older woman. Dong also compares the dramatist with the famous Chinese poet Li Bai [Li Po] (701–62), stating the obvious: 'Li Bai's poems are subjective while Shakespeare's plays present dramatic characters.' Shakespeare's techniques of stagecraft interest him as well, as do devices such as cross-dressing. Dong's other essays focus on specific plays, for example *Julius Caesar* and *Romeo and Juliet*.

Despite Dong's pioneering work, however, it is not until the thirties that serious criticism of Shakespeare really begins in China. Zhang Yuanchang's 1933 article is among the first, considering the authorship question and comparing the rather limited Chinese Shakespeare commentary with criticism of the famous eighteenth-century novel *A Dream of Red Mansions* [*Hongloumeng*].[40] Then, in 1934, scholar and translator Liang Shiqiu answers leftist critic Yan Dunren's dismissive comments about Shakespeare and *The Merchant of Venice* in an essay praising the poet and the play (Meng, *Criticism*: 57–61).

A glance at Liang's piece is in order. First of all, the professor objects to Yan's notion of a Marxist, 'class struggle' approach to Shakespeare. Acknowledging that the playwright may indeed belong 'to the bourgeoisie', Liang argues, 'it doesn't necessarily

---

[39] Abridged in Meng Xianqiang, ed., *Shakespeare Criticism in China*, Changchun: Jilin Education Press, 1991: 52–57.

[40] Cao Xuegin, *A Dream of Red Mansions* [*Hongloumeng*], translated by Yang Hsien-yi and Gladys Yang, 3 vols., Beijing: Foreign Languages Press, 1978–80. Another notable complete English translation of the novel is titled *The Story of the Stone*, 5 vols.; the first three volumes translated by David Hawkes, the last two by John Minford (Harmondsworth: Penguin Books, 1973–86).

follow that all his works were written to benefit his own class'. He judiciously observes that in general we can only guess at Shakespeare's real intentions in his plays. Turning to *The Merchant of Venice*, the play at hand, Liang notes that it is 'a comedy in form' but with 'the heaviness of a tragedy'. Seeing justification in Shylock's actions and attempts at revenge, Liang feels that the Jew 'deserves our compassion. . . . Frankly, except for Portia, Shylock is the most decent character in the play.' Further, Liang views the Christians' persecution of Shylock as 'a good mocking of Christianity'. Why, the critic asks, don't the supposed friends of Antonio immediately come to the merchant's rescue by loaning him the money to pay back Shylock? Liang concludes, 'Shakespeare does not stand on Shylock's side and he does not stand on Antonio's side either. He only objectively depicts a conflict, and the emotions of the characters on both sides of this conflict. Shakespeare did not represent any class; what he represented was humanity.' In these early years of Shakespeare in China, Professor Liang Shiqiu, in addition to the work on his *Complete Shakespeare*, had his critical say on many of the plays, and also found time to translate important commentary by foreign scholars and critics.

Another significant essay from the mid-thirties is John C.H. Wu's 'Shakespeare as a Taoist'[41]. Wu believes Shakespeare's 'Lavish and profuse . . . music' strikes the 'one key-note of Taoism'. He explains, 'The fundamental of Taoism is the subtle idea of the permeation or interpenetration of opposites, life's mingled yarn, . . . [and] This is exactly the vision that Shakespeare saw.' Furthermore, Wu argues, 'Shakespeare is so inebriated with this thoroughly Taoist notion that he applies it to every situation in life, with the result that underneath the infinite variety of his lore, there lurks a simplicity that is primordial.' In sum Wu declares, 'I almost think that the works of Shakespeare can be used as a casebook of Taoism.' Sentimental and impressionistic though it is – that is, long on sweeping and unsubstantiated generalizations and

---

[41] 'Shakespeare as a Taoist', *T'ien Hsia Monthly* 3 (1936): 116–36.

juxtapositions but short on careful and convincing analysis – Wu's study does, on the other hand, look 'at Shakespeare through Chinese eyes', and makes an early attempt to 'understand Shakespeare in a Chinese way'. However, Wu's essay is rather unique. He Qixin, writing as late as 1986, contends that the 'mainstream in Chinese interpretation of Shakespeare is not primarily the result of . . . traditional Chinese concepts; it has little to do with China's past'[42]. Indeed, even early on it often had a political and ideological agenda.

Perhaps the most significant essay from the forties in terms of later Marxist criticism is Yang Hui's 'Preface' to his 1944 translation of *Timon of Athens* (Meng, *Criticism*: 82–101). Cao Weifeng calls it 'the first and most important critical essay on Shakespeare's works from a Marxist-Leninist approach' (quoted in Meng, *Survey*: 26). This detailed study of a play mentioned a number of times in the writings of Marx and Engels anticipates the critical slant that became *de rigueur* for Chinese critics on the mainland after 1949. Yang first rehearses well-known facts about Shakespeare's life and times, reading the playwright's presumed biography into the critic's interpretation of Elizabeth's and James' reigns. Yang discusses the waning of feudalism and the initial optimism about the new social order replacing it, likening the social chaos at the start of the seventeenth century to a 'corresponding situation in [contemporary] China: the old moral order was bankrupt and the new moral order had yet to be established'. Then Yang launches into his interpretation of *Timon of Athens*, suggesting that 'the play is Shakespeare's violent attack on his society, his roar of anger' at what had happened in England after the death of Elizabeth. Gold was the corrupter and enemy: '*Timon of Athens* is the tragedy of Gold.' While admitting that the play is artistically inferior to a *Hamlet* or *King Lear,* Yang nonetheless emphatically states that *Timon* 'is Shakespeare's most important work. If we want to know Shakespeare, his era and society, we need to study the play.' This

---

[42] 'Shakespeare Through Chinese Eyes', Ph.D. dissertation: Kent State University, OH, 1986: 45. (Abbreviated as *STCE* hereafter.)

bold and perhaps extravagant statement about a play that is most often dismissed as inferior and minor Shakespeare reflects an interpretation that is clearly grounded in Marxist-Leninist ideological assumptions.

* * *

In conclusion, it is important to remember that before 1949 much of the enormous population of China, more than eighty per cent of whom were peasants, was uneducated and illiterate, and thus readers of Shakespeare were few and far between. It was also very difficult for people to see Shakespeare performed, for productions were done mostly in the major cities and for select and limited audiences. Add to this anti-foreign feeling, virulent at times in the first half of the twentieth century – calls for boycotts of Western products, general suspicion of things foreign, and civil and international wars – and one can see that Shakespeare held a very tenuous place in China from 1903 to 1949. Without the English and American missionaries and foreign study by Chinese intellectuals, Shakespeare might have arrived in the Middle Kingdom much later than he actually did.

CHAPTER TWO

Shakespeare and Mao, 1 October 1949–1966

'. . . I slide/O'er sixteen years . . .' (*The Winter's Tale* IV, i, 5–6)

Toward the end of her book *On Photography*, Susan Sontag describes Chinese picture taking: 'Not only are there proper subjects for the camera, those which are positive, inspirational (exemplary activities, smiling people, bright weather), and orderly, but there are proper ways of photographing . . .' Private snapshots as well as public images, she notes, are usually posed and conventional. There are no candid photographs, close-ups, or odd-angle shots. In the People's Republic of China in particular, most photography seems to be what foreigners have come to associate with the magazine *China Today* (formerly *China Reconstructs*) – happy and sunny propaganda images. Sontag concludes: 'For the Chinese . . . there are only clichés – which they consider not to be clichés but "correct views" '[1]. Even up to the present time, these 'correct views' are true for Shakespeare in the People's Republic of China as well as for photography.

There are two well-defined periods of Shakespeare activity since the 1 October 1949 founding of the PRC. The first dates to the mid-sixties and the second is roughly from 1978 to the present.

---

[1] *On Photography*, New York: Anchor Books, 1990: 170–3.

The intervening time is the era of the Great Proletariat Cultural Revolution, when almost all Shakespeare activity ceased. Additionally, various other anti-foreign campaigns during the more open years also affected Shakespeare study, translation, production, and criticism. Several of Mao Zedong's important statements, first offered in speeches and later edited and published, sometimes with significant changes, shaped Chinese attitudes regarding foreign literature in general and Shakespeare in particular. Together with Mao's dictates, Soviet Marxist criticism during the first decade of Communist rule in China, and even after the PRC's break with the USSR in 1960, influenced and were models for Chinese Shakespeare scholars and theatre practitioners up to and, for many, even into the new millennium.

Background

Eleanor Marx recalls, 'As to Shakespeare he was the Bible of our house, seldom out of our hands or mouths. By the time I was six I knew scene upon scene of Shakespeare by heart.'[2] Throughout her father's and Frederick Engels' voluminous writings, Shakespeare is liberally referred to, paraphrased, and quoted. For example, in Volume 1 of the *Collected Works of Marx and Engels*, Karl Marx quotes lines from *Hamlet, Julius Caesar, Henry IV (1 and 2), King Lear, Richard III, The Merchant of Venice, A Midsummer Night's Dream, Othello,* and *Troilus and Cressida*. In Volume 2, Engels writes of Shakespeare's 'divine comedies', and in Volume 3 Marx uses passages from *Timon of Athens* to discuss the power of money (*Marx and Engels*: 100; 322–26). As early as 1934 the leftist writer Mao Dun (1896–1982), writing as Wei Ming, published 'Shakespeare

---

[2] Quoted in *Marx and Engels on Literature and Art*, eds. Lee Baxandall and Stefan Thorowski, St. Louis: Telos Press, 1983: 147. (*Marx and Engels* hereafter.) See also R.S. White, 'Marx and Shakespeare', *Shakespeare Survey 45*, ed. Stanley Wells, Cambridge: Cambridge University Press, 1993: 89–101.

and Realism', the first Chinese essay to remark Marx and Engel's interest in Shakespeare, and also the first to discuss Soviet Shakespeare studies.[3]

By the time of the Chinese Communist victory on the mainland in 1949, Russian culture had long embraced Shakespeare. In the eighteenth century, for example, Catherine the Great, that obsessive collector and patron of the arts, freely translated *The Merry Wives of Windsor* (1786) and adapted *Timon of Athens*. Shakespeare influenced Pushkin in *Boris Godunov* (1825), *Count Nulin* (1825), and *Angelo* (1833). Both Turgenev and Dostoevsky admired Shakespeare, and the combative Tolstoy argued with his ideas. As might be expected, during the early years of the Soviet era Shakespeare was vigorously attacked, but in turn the likes of Maxim Gorky and other respected writers and intellectuals came to his defence. To Alexander Smirnov, a leading Soviet Shakespeare scholar and Leningrad University professor, the playwright wrote from the point of view of the emerging bourgeoisie, but nonetheless criticized bourgeois ideology and implicitly advocated the coming revolution in England.[4] The Soviets felt that Shakespeare was held in higher esteem in their country than in the English-speaking world, America for instance. Chinese Shakespearean Huang Zuolin noted, 'On Broadway only one of Shakespeare's plays (*Henry VIII*) was produced in 1948. In Soviet Russia, Shakespeare is almost a daily affair. Apart from conferences and festivals held in his honor every year since 1939 ... Shakespeare is being played to packed houses not only in Moscow and Leningrad, but in the regional theatres as well.'[5]

---

[3] Mao Dun [Wei Ming], 'Shakespeare and Realism', *Wen shi* [*Literature and History*] 1:3 (1934): 81–83. (See Meng, *Survey*: 15–16). Mao Dun, who became the PRC's Minister of Culture after 1949, wrote the celebrated novel *Midnight*, about the corrupt and capitalistic Shanghai in the thirties.

[4] See Alexander Smirnov, 'Shakespeare: A Marxist Interpretation', *Approaches to Shakespeare*, ed. Norman Rabkin, New York: McGraw-Hill, 1964: 160–71.

[5] 'Producing Shakespeare in China', *Chinese Literature* 4 (Winter 1984): 210.

Although a number of Soviet scholars and critics served as models for Chinese Shakespeareans during the early years of the PRC, two seem especially notable: Mikhail Morozov and Alexander Anikst. Moscow University professor Morozov's credentials included representing the USSR on *Shakespeare Survey's* 'Panel of Correspondents', and he also contributed to that journal's early volumes. His many books include *Commentaries on Shakespeare's Plays* (1941) and *Shakespeare on the Soviet Stage* (1947). His study *Shakespeare in the Soviet Union* was translated twice into Chinese during the fifties. Morozov's countryman Anikst was co-editor (with the aforementioned Alexander Smirnov) of a complete Russian language Shakespeare (eight volumes, 1957–60), and his *Shakespeare and his Plays* was also translated into Chinese in the fifties. In the eighties, Anikst's biography of Shakespeare (1964) received a Chinese translation as well.[6] Additionally, a number of articles by both Morozov and Anikst were printed in the 1963 Chinese anthology *Reference Materials for Foreign Literature*.[7]

Like Smirnov, his Marxist compatriot, Morozov felt that Shakespeare anticipated the 'bourgeois revolution' which overthrew the English monarchy in the seventeenth century (see He, *STCE*: 13–14). Failure to perceive this motif in Shakespeare's plays, Morozov contends, results in failure to understand the playwright's underlying message. Taking his cues from Marx and Engels, Morozov points to Shakespeare's attacks on money worship, the 'poison' of capitalism, in *Romeo and Juliet* and *Timon of Athens*. He stresses what he considers the playwright's 'realism' (that is, Shakespeare's theme of the ongoing struggle among the classes and the oppression of the masses), a point picked up by many Chinese critics. Morozov argues that 'Shakespeare . . .

---

[6] Alexander Anikst, *Biography of Shakespeare*, Trans. by An Guoliang, Beijing: Zhongguo xiju chubanshe, 1984.

[7] See, He Qixin, 'Major Trends of Shakespeare Criticism in China', *Proceedings of the Patristic, Mediaeval and Renaissance Conference* [at Villanova University] 9 (1984): 100, n. 7.

always portrayed contemporary [Elizabethan and Jacobean] life in his plays although his characters often assumed different costumes, for instance, the Italian costume in *Romeo and Juliet* and *Othello*, the ancient Danish in *Hamlet*, the ancient British in *King Lear*, and the ancient Scottish in *Macbeth*' (quoted in He, *STCE*: 13).[8]

Anikst, too, sees Shakespeare from the viewpoint of Marxist ideology. He argues that the plays expressed progressive views and were written especially for the masses.[9] Anikst views *Hamlet* as 'a social tragedy ... [because] it not only concerns the conflict between the protagonist and the injustice and sufferings inflicted upon him but also presents a protest against the injustice and evils of the world' (quoted in He, *STCE*: 13). Anikst goes on to argue that Hamlet is a people's hero whose task is to free the oppressed masses.

Chinese critics attempted early on to assimilate the ideas and follow the analytical models of their 'elder brothers' the Soviets, and perhaps not surprisingly Marxist approaches to Shakespeare dominate in the PRC even to this day. As might be expected, they emphasize historical and socioeconomic issues, class relationships, and various critiques of feudalism, capitalism, and religion ('superstition'). Shakespeare's own ideological status and orthodoxy is a matter for interpretation, as Chinese critics focus on what they see as the class struggle prompting a given work during England's early modern period and/or the class struggle represented in a play or group of plays.

---

[8] See also Mikhail Morozov, 'On the Dynamism of Shakespeare's Characters', *Shakespeare in the Soviet Union: A Collection of Articles*, trans. Avril Pyman, eds. Roman Samarin and Alexander Nikolyukin, Moscow, 1966: 113–40.

[9] Anikst suggests that Shakespeare is 'the people's poet', and hence exploits folk tradition; he expresses progressive tendencies, although he is clearly not a revolutionary.

Mao on Art

The Russian critic Anatoli Lunacharsky (1875–1933) coined the phrase 'socialist realism' to describe a theatre that should, in his view, accompany revolution. He advocated a 'new realism', one that reflected the lives of ordinary people and described contemporary class-oriented society. 'Socialist realism', however, was seen by many as little more than a theatre of Marxist political propaganda. On the other hand, Mao Zedong, as reflected in his influential 1942 'Talks at the Yenan Forum on Art and Literature' (63–93), subscribed to Lunacharsky's view. Mao's seminal ideological essay, referred to by one scholar as 'the supreme treatise on literary criticism in China',[10] came to be a guide to orthodoxy for Chinese Shakespeareans, as well as other critics, scholars, and creative writers. Mao announces as his subject, 'the proper relationship between our work in the artistic and literary fields and our revolutionary work in general' ('Talks': 63). He is especially concerned with the appropriate audience, the 'for whom', of literature and art. Mao writes that in revolutionary China there is no room for 'elitist art', subjective 'art for art's sake', which in his view serves 'the exploiters and oppressors'. All literature and art should be 'for the masses' – that is, for 'workers, peasants, and soldiers'. Mao states, Chinese writers should 'conscientiously learn the language of the masses', and he mandates a readily comprehensible, ideological-focused art. At some later and rather unspecific moment, when the masses have been sufficiently educated and ready for it, art can be developed into a more elevated and sophisticated expression. Although Mao would have his revolutionary artists and writers learn from foreign practice and the past, he puts Chinese Shakespeare scholars, critics, and theatre people on notice: 'We must take over all the fine artistic and literary legacy, critically assimilate from it *whatever is beneficial to us* [italics mine] and hold it up as an example when we try to work

---

[10] Wang Shuhua, 'Politics into Play: Shakespeare in Twentieth-Century China', Ph.D. dissertation: The Pennsylvania State University, 1993: 4.

over the artistic and literary raw material derived from the people's life of our own time and place' ('Talks': 76). His summary note contains a clear warning: 'Experts should be respected; they are very valuable to our cause. But we should also remind them that no revolutionary artist or writer can produce any work of significance unless he has contact with the masses, gives expression to their thoughts and feelings, and becomes their loyal spokesman' ('Talks': 80). Shakespeare critics, scholars, and theatre people, it follows, must interpret the playwright/poet to serve the ideological and political objectives of the present and ongoing revolution.

This same utilitarian approach is also evident in Mao's 1956 'Talk to the Music Workers'.[11] In this lecture Mao states, 'We must learn many things from foreign countries and master them.' As an example, Mao cites Lu Xun's *nalaizhuyi* ['taking the foreign']. He argues that Lu assimilated the valuable in Western learning in order to utilize it in his own uniquely Chinese way. To the musicians, Mao again stresses the remolding and re-education of intellectuals so that they will support wholeheartedly the revolutionary cause.

Mao's other important statement for would-be Chinese Shakespeareans is contained in 'On the Correct Handling of Contradictions Among the People'.[12] The Chinese leader first offered this lecture in 1957, but revised it for publication to take a harder line because the speech version yielded unanticipated and unwelcome results. While this lecture, too, was not specifically about foreign literature and criticism, it encouraged intellectuals to express themselves freely – as Mao put it, 'let a hundred flowers blossom and a hundred schools of thought contend'. What transpired was that many academics and other intellectuals took Mao at his word, and attacked, among other things, corruption in the

---

[11] *Mao Tse-tung on Art and Literature*, Peking: Foreign Languages Press, 1960: 84–90.

[12] *Communist China, 1955–1959: Policy Documents with Analysis*, Cambridge, MA: Harvard University Press, 1962: 273–94.

government, the Chinese Communist Party, and even the leadership itself. Consequently, the revised published version of 'Contradictions', in a section titled 'The Question of Intellectuals',
included the following statement: 'Not to have a correct political
point of view is like having no soul', a clear signal that in Mao's
mind there were both 'fragrant flowers and poisonous weeds'.
Mao warns:

> Most of our intellectuals have made marked progress during
> the past seven years. They express themselves in favour of the
> socialist system. Many of them are diligently studying Marxism,
> and some have become Communists. Their number, though
> small, is growing steadily. There are, of course, still some intel-
> lectuals who are skeptical of socialism or who do not approve
> of it, but they are in a minority … They must continue to
> remould themselves, gradually shed their bourgeois world
> outlook.[13]

Shakespeareans were thereby once again alerted to the fact that
their approach to the playwright and his plays must follow and
reinforce the party line.

In his three lectures Mao spells out a view of the utilitarian
function of art that must be aimed at the masses, and in turn the
interpretation and *analyses* of art should also be directed at the majority population. Since Mao, the thoroughgoing Marxist, believed
that all art derives from class divisions and reinforces class prejudices, it cannot therefore contain universal truths. Clearly con-
sumed by revolutionary fervour and guided by political ideology,
Mao's propagandistic programme for Chinese literature and criticism is not at all concerned with aesthetic issues, perhaps ironic in
a poet who allowed his own artful poetry based on traditional
Chinese forms to be collected and published in 1957.[14]

---

[13] Ibid.: 286.
[14] See a selection in English translation by Hualing Nieh Engle and Paul
Engle, *Poems of Mao Tse-tung*, New York: Dell, 1972.

Shakespeare Commentary

As we have mentioned, Shakespeare's own ideological orthodoxy was a matter for interpretation. The playwright receives praise for his realism, humanism, and attacks on feudalism, but he is also criticized for his negative view of the masses (in, say, *Julius Caesar* and *Coriolanus*) and his harsh treatment of women characters in several plays (for example, in *The Taming of the Shrew* and *Othello*). Chinese scholars, too, focused on what they took to be clues to Shakespeare's revolutionary stance in the few known details of his life and/or in a given work or group of works. In this early period, their criticism and analyses were largely unsophisticated, simplistic, and reductionist Marxism, and careful to kowtow to Mao's dictates as well.[15] They began with common knowledge about Shakespeare and given Marxist assumptions. For example, Li Funing, writing about *As You Like It* in 1956, relates the play to pastoral and satiric literature and Robin Hood folklore, but also sees this comedy as Shakespeare's analysis of the English society of his time.[16] He first considers the materialism of the late sixteenth century, where 'money and profit' were the order of the day and many lived in cruel poverty. Li next looks at Shakespeare's sources for *As You Like It*, finding the Robin Hood narratives especially relevant because the Sherwood Forest hero 'fought the ruling class and their running dogs' [*sic*]. Li contends that Shakespeare is 'anti-feudalist' and 'anti-capitalist', and that

---

[15] Wang Shuhua notes this about Chinese Marxist critics: 'It is . . . [their] didactic, utilitarian emphasis – ethics and pragmatism – that distinguishes the Chinese Marxist critic from Marxist critics in other communist or Western societies. Literary values have never been truly separated from pragmatic values in China. In the Mao era, economic and political concerns all but wiped out literary values, and Shakespearean criticism became a combined exercise of Maoist ideology and traditional Chinese ethics which proves to be an age-old burden too heavy even for the Great Helmsman to shake off' ('Politics': 48).

[16] '*As You Like It*', reprinted in Meng, *Criticism*: 159–83.

he uses satire (for example, in the comments of Touchstone and Jacques) to point out contemporary social problems. While Jacques' melancholy may be an aristocratic pose, Li argues that the majority of people in early modern England had a real reason to be melancholy due to the society's injustices. Li concludes his essay as follows: '[*As You Like It*] helps us understand how the intense social conflicts profoundly altered the way Shakespeare perceived the world, how his plays changed from comedy to tragedy, and how his humanist views progressed from the fantasy of pastoral idealism to harsh criticism of the evils of English society at a time of the primitive accumulation of capital' (Meng, *Criticism*: 181–82). This seems a lot of historical weight to put on a play that is, in the end, a romantic comedy mostly about love.

Again in 1956, Nanjing University professor and Yale Ph.D. Chen Jia [Carl Chia Chen] published a pioneering essay suggesting that Shakespeare's political views are revealed in his history plays as well.[17] He argues the playwright's own life and the social background of his times greatly influenced his attitudes. Chen sees Shakespeare as belonging to the progressive bourgeois class that helped bring about the collapse of feudalism in England. While on the one hand Shakespeare supports the monarchy, he is against strongly centralized power, and his ideal king is one who promotes equality, has the people's interests at heart, observes the country's laws, and is able to extend national territory. Chen views Henry V as Shakespeare's ideal king, and notes the insistent patriotism in all the history plays. This patriotism, however, is a counterpoint to the individual pursuit of selfish interests, especially when it comes to money. Falstaff's 'press', the nobles' betrayal of King Henry to the French, and Falconbridge's 'commodity speech' are among the examples Chen cites as evidence. He writes, 'The dialogues and monologues about the worship of gold were not from Holinshed or any other source, but a reflection of

---

[17] 'Shakespeare's Political Views Revealed in His Historical Plays', reprinted in Meng, *Criticism*: 141–58.

the playwright's deep consciousness of the prevalence of the thought in the then British society.' Chen concludes:

> Shakespeare obviously revealed his own political views in his history plays. He was against feudal separation, tyrants, and civil war. He was for centralization of power, national unity, and a just king. He hated the conflicts between the monarch and nobles because they brought disaster to the country. He noticed the significant power of the bourgeois and the working people (especially the towns' people). He exposed, although in a limited way, the oppression and exploitation of aristocrats against the people (including the bourgeois). He applauded patriotism and criticized the unscrupulous pursuit of personal interest. His attitudes were from the middle class viewpoint, but also often reflected the voice of the working people. One thing is worthy of special note: he criticized the ugliness of the bourgeois class. This fact reflected the progressiveness of Shakespeare and his standing on the same ground as the common people.

Bian Zhilin, arguably the most important scholar/translator of this early PRC period, uses *Hamlet* to express similar Marxist views.

In the late thirties, Bian taught at the Lu Xun Arts and Literature Academy [*Lu Xun yishu wenxue yuan*] in Yenan, the Communist base, and later held a professorship at Nankai University. In 1947 the British Council offered him a place as a visiting scholar at Oxford, and later when Bian returned to China he focused on Shakespeare at The Literary Research Institute to Study Chinese and Foreign Literature (established in 1953 by the Academy of Science). Bian writes in the 'Preface' to his 1956 translation of *Hamlet*, which includes a detailed critical analysis of the play, that Shakespeare's tragedy expresses the playwright's progressive views through his plot and characters (Meng, *Criticism*: 120–40). When Hamlet says, 'Denmark's a prison', Bian argues, 'Shakespeare, speaking the innermost thought of Hamlet, here generalizes the realities of the England of his day.' Although the playwright clearly belongs to the emerging middle class, he transcends its limitations. After all, continues Bian, 'The good side of society [with which Shakespeare sympathized] lay obviously with the injured and insulted, in the masses of the people.' Bian sees Hamlet, and thus Shakespeare, clearly on the side of characters such as Horatio, the sentinels, and gravediggers, as opposed to Claudius, Polonius, and the other aristocratic types. On a more general note, and a point often made by other Chinese Shakespeare critics, Bian asserts that 'Shakespeare's age was a transition period between the collapse of feudalism and the rise of capitalism in England.' This, he contends, results in a 'contradiction' between Renaissance humanism and the 'essentially feudalistic' monarchic system reflected in *Hamlet*.

Bian Zhilin wrote another important essay during the fifties, this time considering *Othello*. It similarly stresses Shakespeare's 'realism', 'humanism', and Marxist motifs. Yet again one can observe that reading Shakespeare's supposed ideological beliefs into his works was the order of the day for Chinese scholars and critics. During the decade of the fifties, this kind of Shakespeare commentary was especially energetic. And Shakespeare was the only foreign dramatist 'studied in depth in China' at this time.[18]

* * *

Although relations between the PRC and the USSR broke off in 1960, Soviet models for Chinese Shakespeare criticism were still rigorously followed thereafter. These Russian studies, as the Chinese essays that aped them, continued to focus on the playwright's supposed representations of life in early modern England, regardless of the play or play settings, Shakespeare's anticipation of the coming bourgeois revolution, and his condemnation of capitalist materialism, among other Marxist motifs. Soviet Shakespeare studies were also prominent among the eighty-or-so foreign commentaries translated and published into

---

[18] Norman J. Wilkinson, 'Shakespeare in China', *New England Theatre Journal* 2:1 (1991): 44.

the sixties, a time when a stated leadership priority was the education and integration of intellectuals into the 'new' socialist China.

In a detailed essay on *The Merchant of Venice*, Fan Shen highlights two articles from the early sixties concerning the comedy.[19] Wu Xinghua's 1963 article argues that Shakespeare's view of class struggle cannot automatically be assumed by reading his plays, yet the playwright's social ideology is made clear by carefully studying the changes he made to his sources. For example, Shakespeare expanded the roles of Antonio and Shylock in *Merchant*, as compared with the characters in his *Il Pecorone* source, in order to emphasize and criticize the commercialism of his day. Wu would have Shakespeare both as a bourgeois apologist for his society and as an objective observer who distanced himself from it. Zhao Shouyin and Long Wenpei's 1964 essay attacked Wu, suggesting that he wrongly positions Shakespeare beyond class and history. They conclude, in Fan's translation, 'Wu is insufficiently Maoist both in his criticism of Shakespeare and in his selection of and dependence on Western non-Maoist critics' (Fan, 'Shakespeare': 25–28).

Translations

During the period from the founding of the PRC to roughly 1964, more than a half-million Shakespeare translations were printed on the mainland (Meng, *Survey*: 30). Some represented reissues of earlier work, such as Zhang Caizhen's 1927 version of *As You Like It* or Cao Yu's *Romeo and Juliet* (with some 31,000 copies in print by 1962). Cao Weifeng also revised play translations he had published earlier, and in 1954 brought out a comprehensive critical survey of Chinese Shakespeare translations.[20] In 1954 as well,

---

[19] 'Shakespeare in China: *The Merchant of Venice*', *Asian Theatre Journal* 5:1 (1988): 23–37.

[20] Cao Weifeng, 'Shakespeare in China', *Wenyi yuebao* [*Art and Literature Monthly*] (April 1954): 29–34. (*Wenyi* hereafter.)

Zhu Shenghao's *Collected Plays of Shakespeare* [*Shashibiya xiju*] appeared in twelve volumes, and included the first translations of *1* and *2 Henry IV*, *Richard II*, and *King John*. To meet the great demand, this edition was reprinted numerous times subsequently. In addition, eight scholars were commissioned to render the plays and poetry not completed by Zhu, with the view of offering a new and carefully revised and edited *Complete Works* to celebrate the Bard's 400th birthday in 1964. Due to the turmoil that led ultimately to the Cultural Revolution, however, publication wasn't realized until fourteen years later.

Supplementing the newly translated history plays mentioned above, other notable translations accomplished before the Cultural Revolution included Tu An's version of 'The Sonnets' (1950); Fang Ping's *Much Ado About Nothing* (1953), *The Merchant of Venice* (1954), *Venus and Adonis* (1954), and *Henry V* (1955); Lu Ying's *A Midsummer Night's Dream* (1954); Bian Zhilin's *Hamlet* (1956); and Wu Xinghua's *1* and *2 Henry IV* (1957). But the window of opportunity for Shakespeare translators along with critics closed by the middle sixties.

* * *

To be sure, there are numerous difficulties faced by all of Shakespeare's Chinese translators. Many are obvious: the language dissimilarities, how to suggest iambic pentameter verse, whether to be strictly literal or rather attempt to capture something of the playwright's cleverness and word play, and so on. Moreover, following the establishment of the 'New China', Marxist political and ideological issues, perhaps not surprisingly, come forcefully into play in Shakespeare translation. He Qixin observes, 'The rigid limitations of this political view of Shakespeare's plays riddle the work of critic-translators … not only infecting their understanding of the plays, but their rendition of Shakespeare into Chinese' (He, *STCE*: 148). He adds: 'their inadequate interpretation of Shakespeare's plays, as reflected in their critical essays', often makes their translations 'unfaithful renditions of the original' (He, *STCE*: 126). Fang Ping and Bian Zhilin are among the translators singled out for criticism in He Qixin's master's thesis and doctoral dissertation.

Productions

After the communist victory on the mainland, Mao allocated resources to establish many drama schools and theatrical troupes. Li Ruru estimates that there were more than 160 professional theatre companies founded in the PRC before 1966, employing some 20,000 'workers' ('Bard': 62). In addition to the theatre's entertainment value, Mao recognized that drama had both educational and propagandistic potential. Li observes,

> Shakespeare was taken as representative of progressive humanism, and productions of his plays were expected to bring out the social and economic background of Elizabethan times – especially the emergence of the new bourgeoisie from the feudal structure of the Middle Ages. As the moral was always that brightness had finally overcome darkness, all the leading roles in these productions were monumentally portrayed and stereotyped: the symbol of the progressive forces of the Renaissance ('Bard': 63).

Most Chinese Shakespeare productions during the early years of the PRC were in the two most populous cities. In Shanghai in 1950, the Shaoxing Opera Troupe offered an adaptation of *Othello* (with the altered title that translates *Princess and Lord*), and Beijing's Central Academy of Drama staged the balcony scene from *Romeo and Juliet* to mark Shakespeare's April, 1953 anniversary. Also at the Central Academy, the most significant production of the fifties took place in 1956. Dan Ni (also known as Jin Runzhi) co-directed (with the Soviet Kurinev) a *Romeo and Juliet* that represented the first 'complete' Shakespeare text acted for PRC audiences. Premier Zhou Enlai attended the play's premiere, and posed for pictures with the company following this opening night performance. The production also received a photo spread in the *Illustrated London News*. Particularly remarked was Tian Hua, the actress playing Juliet, who was 'said to have a wide knowledge of the plays' of Shakespeare (13 October 1956: 615).

Dan Ni and her husband Huang Zuolin, both important Chinese Shakespeareans, had studied for a time in England, and also were among the first PRC theatre people sent to the USSR to observe Stanislavsky's techniques. Upon their return from Soviet Russia, they taught the 'method', as did various Russian directors and actors invited to come to the PRC. While Chinese theatre artists concerned with modern drama welcomed the new Stanislavsky approach, there was lively debate among them as to how traditional Chinese drama conventions and stage techniques were to be adapted to fit the Russian's 'fourth wall' realism and method acting. In many ways classical Chinese theatre was antithetical to the new methodology, but, on the other hand, the foreigner Shakespeare could be played around with to produce a sort of intercultural stew.

In 1957 Y.C. Lipkovskaya directed a *Much Ado About Nothing* at the Shanghai Institute of Drama, and this production's optimism and topical relevance was consistent with the freer Chinese spirit of the times (Li, 'Bard': 62). The combination of production topically together with adaptation of the play text henceforth became the preferred model for much of PRC stage Shakespeare.

In the late fifties, several *Twelfth Nights* were also staged. Zhou Enlai attended a 1957 production at the Beijing Film Academy which was, again, inspired by Stanislavsky. Premier Zhou, this time together with Mao himself, received the Shanghai Amateur Theatrical Studio Troupe's cast after a *Twelfth Night* that entertained the Eighth Congress of the Seventh Plenary Session of the Chinese Communist Party. In 1959 the Theatrical Troupe of the Beijing Studio performed yet another *Twelfth Night*.

It was also in the fifties that movie theatres began to screen foreign films of Shakespeare's plays, with subtitles or dubbing in Chinese. Russian versions, such as Sergei Yutkevitch's lushly romantic *Othello* and Yakov Fried's energetic *Twelfth Night* (both 1955), and Laurence Olivier's celebrated *Hamlet* (1948) were all very popular. The *Hamlet* used Bian Zhilin's translation, and was given the new title *The Story of the Prince's Revenge* [*Wangzi fuchouji*].

The early sixties saw *Twelfth Night* mounted yet again by the inaugural graduating class of the Shanghai Film School. In 1961 Zhang Qihong, who had studied at the Moscow Art Theatre, directed a *Romeo and Juliet* for the graduating class of The Central Academy of Drama. In the same year, the Shanghai Youth Art Theatre performed *Much Ado About Nothing*. But by 1964, the 400th anniversary of Shakespeare's birth, the sky darkened and the political weather changed considerably. In that year, the Shanghai People's Art Theatre had been rehearsing *Romeo and Juliet* and the Shanghai Drama Institute *The Merchant of Venice*, but both productions never saw the public stage. The Chinese censorship curtain began to descend on Shakespeare with a 5 January 1964 piece in *Liberation*, a government controlled Shanghai paper. Suggesting that 'old' Shakespeare 'would be ashamed of what he has written', the article continued: 'To suppose that Shakespeare is some sort of god who cannot be surpassed is to lose direction and proceed contrary to the spirit of this epoch and our people.' A January 21 piece followed, containing a harsh warning note: 'Anyone who kneels before the shrine of . . . Shakespeare or other artists and writers is guilty of favoring moribund capitalism.'[21] Defying the warnings, Chen Jia and his Nanjing University students celebrated Shakespeare's special birthday in 1964 by acting scenes in English from *King Lear*, *The Merchant of Venice*, *Hamlet*, and even *Julius Caesar* with its gullible masses. But the professor paid dearly for this politically incorrect breach in later 'struggle sessions' geared to his public humiliation. It was the eve of the Cultural Revolution.

It could be argued perhaps that Gonzalo's Edenic vision in *The Tempest* (II, i, 148–69) holds something in common with the Marxist–Leninist–Maoist visions of the ideal society. Even granting this, it is evident in Shakespeare's play that Gonzalo's ideas

---

[21] Quoted in Robert Guillain, *When China Wakes*, New York: Walker, 1965: 237.

suffer from a dangerous naivety. Indeed, the playwright shows us in his romance that the self-serving in human nature gets in the way of realizing Utopias, no matter how much we long for them.

And Mao would prove himself, in the ensuing years, an unforgiving Prospero to the Chinese people.

CHAPTER THREE

The Great Proletariat Cultural Revolution

'. . . a wilderness of tigers' (*Titus Andronicus* III, i, 54)

American Lois Wheeler Snow, wife of journalist Edgar Snow, visited the PRC with her husband in 1970, during some of the darkest days of the so-called Great Proletariat Cultural Revolution. Edgar Snow's book *Red Star Over China* (1937) contained a sympathetic account of Mao Zedong's communist revolution, and made the journalist the 'new' China's special 'friend'. The most important leaders of the PRC government hosted the Snows, who dined with Premier Zhou Enlai and Madam Mao, Jiang Qing. Lois and Edgar Snow stood with Jiang, Mao himself, and other dignitaries high above Tiananmen Square reviewing events during the 1 October, 1970 'National Day' celebrations.

Lois Snow and Madame Mao had something in common: both were actresses with famous husbands. And while Jiang Qing was one of the orchestrators and directors of the Cultural Revolution, Mrs Snow defended it and sang its praises to America and the outside world in her 1972 book *China on Stage: An American Actress in the People's Republic*. In addition to her surprising and enthusiastic defence of the clearly repressive, anti-intellectual Cultural Revolution, Lois Snow's book includes English translations of four, model 'revolutionary operas'. At this distance, one senses that Mrs Snow was unknowingly used by Jiang Qing and her supporters for propaganda purposes in order to further what now seems their bizarre 'cultural' programme, and that the journalist's wife was kept away from and thus ignorant of the horrific 'struggle sessions', campaigns, and persecutions of artists, intellectuals, and many others at this time of terror.

Edward Said writes in 1978, 'It is very easy to argue that knowledge about Shakespeare . . . is not political whereas knowledge about contemporary China . . . is.'[1] It so happens that *in* China the poet/playwright, as a great cultural icon of the West, has always been 'political' – never more so for China than just before the time of Said's comment. Like every other foreign writer, as well as most Chinese not writing 'new proletarian literature' (that is, anti-Japanese, anti-Nationalist party and regime, pro-the suffering masses), Shakespeare was a victim of the political crackdown in effect roughly between 1966 and 1976. The summer of 1966 saw school closings and the cessation of publication of what most in the world would call 'literature'. The only acceptable subject was the peasants' struggle in the countryside, and traditional 'culture' was censored for the following ten years.[2] An article in the journal *Chinese Literature* promulgated the Party view: 'The so-called "Western culture" is nothing but imperialist culture, which is most reactionary, decadent, and vicious.'[3] Thus, Shakespeare was off-limits. Only eight collectively written operas and ballets were permitted on stages in the PRC. The new 'reformed' operas included *Taking Tiger Mountain by Strategy*, *The Red Lantern*, *Shajiabang*, *The Harbour*, *A Surprise Attack on the White Tiger Regiment*; the revolutionary ballets were *The White-Haired Girl* and *The Red Detachment of Women*; and there was also an 'entertainment' of accompanied

---

[1] *Orientalism*, New York: Pantheon, 1978: 9.

[2] Hao Ran's novel *The Broad Road in the Golden Sunlight* [*Jinguang dadao*], published in 1972, would eventually become the model work.

[3] Quoted in Michael Schoenhols, ed., *China's Cultural Revolution, 1966–1969: Not A Dinner Party*, Armonk, NY: M.E. Sharpe, 1996: 269.

song. During this troubled time, writing about, teaching, acting in, discussing, even possessing Shakespeare's work was dangerous and might yield criticism or worse from the youthful Red Guard or the fearful and indoctrinated general population. All Chinese translations of Shakespeare were removed from libraries and bookstores, and stage productions and films of this now clearly 'reactionary writer' were banned. Tian Han, who had chaired the Chinese Drama Association in the fifties and translated the first complete Shakespeare play text, was labelled a 'poisonous weed' and persecuted to his death, as were many other scholars and writers. The Bard's very name was reviled, as the Chinese characters for 'asprin' and *Sha-shi-bi-ya* were purposely confused as a form of ridicule (Meng, *Survey*: 34). Shakespeare did not fit the revolutionary 'one age, one author and one piece of literary work' ideal (He, *STCE*: 20–21, n.35).[4]

The Cultural Revolution began in part as a struggle between an aging Mao Zedong and other powerful leaders for control of the Chinese Communist Party, but then accelerated into a 'continuing revolution' that eventually got out of hand and brought chaos and suffering to all of China (Spence, *Search*: 791). Due in part to short-sighted policies such as the 1958 'Great Leap Forward', as well as the 1960 break with the Soviet Union, 1961 drought and floods resulting in widespread famine, and a variety of other major national setbacks, dramatic new initiatives were needed to rekindle the revolutionary fires of the past and divert attention from recent failures and current problems. The Cultural Revolution was such an initiative.

Many heart-rending accounts of these turbulent times have been written: Nien Cheng's *Life and Death in Shanghai*, Jung Chang's *Wild Swans: Three Daughters of China*, Da Chen's *Color of the Mountain*, Anchee Min's *Red Azalea*, Jan Wong's *Red China Blues* are just a few. Teachers and intellectuals generally, people with Western ties, 'landlords' and their families, and others in specified categor-

---

[4] This was a satirical phrase used by Cultural Revolution critics.

ies suffered devastating 'criticism sessions' and 're-education' that often meant exile to hard labour in the countryside or in factories, prison, or worse. As one Shakespeare scholar writes with some irony, 'in the years of the "Great Proletarian Cultural Revolution", strangely enough, I found myself arraigned on the same bench with Shakespeare, for Shakespeare and I were criticized together' (Ho, 'Shakespeare': 11). This period was one of overwhelming paranoia, but also justifiable fear. Husbands betrayed wives and wives husbands, and children betrayed parents. Many could not endure the pressures of the time, and some committed suicide. No one was safe from attack, even high officials. All looked over their shoulders. It was a period of zealousness, terror, and wanton cultural destruction. Confucian temples and other ancient historical sites and monuments were vandalized with official sanction. In Qufu, Shandong Province, Confucius' tumulus and the graves of some of his descendents were desecrated and dug up, ancient steles smashed.

The youthful Red Guards were the enforcers of Mao's new revolutionary policies. Waving their 'Little Red Books' containing the memorized *Quotations From Chairman Mao*, they often terrorized the general population in their attempts to get rid of the 'four olds' (that is, old ideas, culture, customs, habits). The Chairman gave these high school and university students the task of weeding out 'reactionaries' of all stripes. In turn, the zealous youths questioned and challenged traditional authority, humiliated their teachers, defaced and destroyed important cultural artefacts, and burned books. Looking back on her time as a Red Guard, Liu Yan offers a chilling account of one such book-burning incident:

> Except for those books whose covers featured Chairman Mao's portrait, almost all of the books in the [school] library were removed and carried out to the center of the sports ground by the 'Black Gang' [a designation for 'bourgeois elements' in the school]. Forcing them to do this were my classmates – Red Guards brandishing leather belts with brass buckles. The Red Guards insisted that these books had spread feudalist, capitalist,

and revisionist ideas and that therefore they had to be burned (quoted in Schoenhals, *Revolution*: 327–28).

In another episode, a significant Shakespeare casualty was The Shanghai Drama Institute's carefully preserved copy of the 1913 script of Shakespeare's *Rouquan* (*Flesh Contract* [*The Merchant of Venice*]) (Li, 'Bard': 77, n.7).

The directors and driving force behind what was, in actuality, an *anti*-cultural revolution of intimidation, repression, and censorship was the so-called 'Gang of Four' – Yao Wenyuan, Zhang Chunqiao, Wang Hongwen, and Jiang Qing, Mao's third wife. Madame Mao was clearly ringleader of this 'Gang'. Born in 1914, in her youth she was an aspiring stage and screen actress in Jinan and Shanghai. Using the stage name Lan Ping, she once played the role of Nora in Ibsen's *A Doll's House*. In 1933 she joined the Communist Party, and by 1937 had travelled to Yenan, the communist revolutionary base.[5] While working at the Lu Xun Arts Academy, she met and married Mao in 1939 and bore him two daughters. Relegated to the political wings for a spell, but continually plotting for power, in the early sixties she emerged at centre stage as useful to her husband during his troubled times. As might be expected, Madame Jiang condemned criticism aimed at Mao and the Communist Party in general. But she also had an agenda of her own, one aspect of which was to promote a new kind of Chinese socialist culture. She attacked, for example, what she labelled 'anti-revolutionary art', especially so-called 'ghost plays'. Shakespeare's plays with their witches, supernatural spirits, and religious dimensions and allusions came under this definition. Jiang asserted, 'we are members of the Communist Party, and we absolutely do not believe there are ghosts, spirits, or God in the world' (quoted in Fei, *Theories*: 167). However, it was not Shakespeare but Wu Han's drama *Hairui Dismissed From Office*, a clear allegory attacking Mao's dismissal of Peng Dehuai as

---

[5] Yenan was the headquarters for Mao's Eighth Route Army and its followers from 1937–47, and now is a communist shrine.

Defence Minister, which especially incensed Jiang Qing, and her criticism of this play brought her to special prominence in July of 1962. Wu was Deputy Mayor of Beijing and a scholar of the Ming period, and Madame Mao made him and his play the flash point for launching the Cultural Revolution. Wu ultimately died in prison in 1969, a broken man. Jiang recalled,

> I was very perplexed to find that some seriously counter-revolutionary plays like *Hairui Dismissed from Office* (*Hairui baguan*), *Li Huiniang*, and so on were being produced on the stage of the Beijing opera, an art form that had never been that responsive to social reality. There were also many plays centered around emperors, generals, and ministers, gifted scholars, and beautiful ladies (*diwang, jiangxiang, caizi, jiaren*), all in the legitimate name of 'rediscovering tradition' (quoted in Fei, *Theories*: 167).

But the 'tradition' to Madame Jiang was for an elitist group, so she was determined, as she put it, to 'create a literature and art which [would] protect our socialist economic base'.[6] That is to say, the present should be favoured over the past, the native over the foreign, and every work should promote an acceptable ideology. To this end, she condemned not only Shakespeare and all classical Western drama, popular in China since the early years of the century, but soon even the thought-to-be sacrosanct traditional Beijing Opera (Snow, *Stage*: 8). In 1964 she promoted a festival of so-called 'Beijing Opera on Contemporary Themes'. Her justification was the claim that Chairman Mao had this in mind when he spoke of bringing forth 'new' art from the 'old', and having it serve the workers, peasants, and soldiers. During the Cultural Revolution, the rewritten Beijing opera *Driven to Join the Liang Mountain Rebels* [*Bishang liangshan*] became a model for revamping traditional theatre, in part because it had prompted Mao's effusive

---

[6] Quoted in Lois Wheeler Snow, *China On Stage: An American Actress in the People's Republic*, New York: Vintage Books, 1973: 19.

1944 letter of praise to its authors.[7] Two other Mao speeches, 'On New Democracy' (1940) and 'Speech at the Chinese Communist Party's National Conference on Propaganda Work' (1957), also were cited to justify the new genre and denounce traditional forms (Snow, *Stage*: 15). As for the old opera, Madame Jiang asserted, 'how can we accept, critically or otherwise, the moral codes of the feudal landlord class or the capitalist class, for whom oppression and exploitation were perfectly justified?' (quoted in Fei, *Theories*: 167–68). Thus, model operas and ballets, written by committees under Jiang's direction, with contemporary themes, costumes, sets, and characters, replaced not only traditional opera and ballet, but also every other theatre experience as well, Shakespeare included. The bourgeois Bard was elitist and promoted an evil morality.

Lois Snow describes the new genre as follows: 'Model Chinese opera is neither pure entertainment nor an exposition of factors that explain a complicated character ... the purpose of

---

[7] Mao's letter dated January 9 reads as follows:

Comrades [Yang] Shaoxuan and [Qi] Yanming,

I saw your play; you have done a great job. I thank you, and please tell the actors I thank them! History is created by the people, but on the stage of the old traditional theatre (in the literature and arts that have been separated from the people) the people have been turned into the dregs of society, while the Masters, Madames, Young Masters, and Young Misses have dominated the stage. This reversal of history has now been reversed again by you; you have restored history to its true face, and you have given the old traditional theatre a new beginning. For this I congratulate you. Guo Moruo has done a lot in history plays in the area of spoken drama; now you have done so in the old traditional theatre. What you have begun is an epoch-making beginning of revolutionizing old traditional theatre. I am very pleased when I think of this. Hope you write more and perform more, building up the momentum and making it the order of the day across the land!

With high respect,

Mao Zedong

(Quoted in Fei, *Theories*: 142)

revolutionary drama is to educate on class lines, with the interests of the proletariat foremost in mind' (*Stage*: 249). It is, in other words, primarily communist propaganda. Universal themes, memorable characters, and artistic self-expression, what we might associate with Shakespeare, were considered to be 'against the mainstream of history' and result in 'a bourgeois – and false – concept of art and literature' (Snow, *Stage*: 249). Writers' groups wrote the few acceptable melodramatic 'entertainments', and they were soon promulgated everywhere in China. They, most significantly, had no 'middle characters', realistic and lifelike people, who exhibit both good and bad qualities.[8] Shakespeare, of course, is the master of such characters, and is celebrated for creating so many of them. Model Opera characters, on the other hand, had to be stereotypical heroic soldiers, workers, or peasants; villains were almost exclusively cruel landlords, 'capitalist roaders', or Nationalist puppets. Proletariat suffering, anger, and most of all justifiable revenge as 'justice' constituted the bulk of the not-so-subtle plot lines.

Taking Tiger Mountain by Strategy is a good example of one of the acceptable operas (Snow, *Stage*: 40–98). The head note to the English version suggests that Mao himself edited and approved the text: 'The modern revolutionary Peking opera *Taking Tiger Mountain by Strategy*, carefully revised, perfected and polished to the last detail with our great leader Chairman Mao's loving care, now glitters with surpassing splendour' (Snow, *Stage*: 40). As with traditional Peking opera, dance and song are incorporated into the action. This work, just as all the other operas and ballets of the Cultural Revolution, is an exaggerated melodrama complete with vile villains and model Communist heroes. For example, the bandit gang cruelly exploits the peasants, and the totally depraved

---

[8] Snow defines 'middle characters' as 'a term used for persons in literature and in theatre who are not wholeheartedly dedicated to the principles of Chinese socialism, people "who are midway between good and bad, the positive and negative, the advanced and the backward, people tainted by the 'old things' " ' (*Stage*: 119).

and despicable Bandit Chief even tears a baby from its mother's arms and throws it over a cliff to its death. The outlaws have suggestive names that translate as 'Vulture' and the 'Eight Terribles'. Furthermore, they are in league with the enemy Americans, Chiang Kai-shek and the Kuomintang, as well as other bandit gangs.[9] On the hero's side in the opera are the People's Liberation Army, the Communist Party, Chairman Mao Zedong, and the masses and their representatives.

The PLA, 'winning big victories at the front', announce: 'Neighbors, we are the worker and peasant soldiers. We protect the people.' They sing:

> *We're the worker and peasant soldier, come*
> *To destroy the reactionaries and change the world.*
> *We've fought for years north and south for the revolution,*
> *With the Party and Chairman Mao leading the way,*
> *A red star on our army caps,*
> *Two red flags of the revolution on our collar.*
> *Where the red flag goes dark clouds disperse.*
> *Liberated people overthrow the landlords.*

The 'neighbors' respond in turn: '*These soldiers care for us folks and cure our ailments;/ They're considerate, kind and helpful*' (Snow, *Stage*: 74–78).

An arm of the Communist Party, the PLA is 'helping the poor to win emancipation' (Snow, *Stage*: 47). Yang Tzu-jung, the model hero of the drama, has an appropriate family background and history. He was '*Born of a hired-hand peasant family,/ From childhood he struggled on the brink of death;/* . . . [but] *found his salvation/ In the Communist Party and took the revolutionary road*' (Snow, *Stage*: 59). Thus, when tested Yang sings, '*A Communist always heeds the Party's call,/* . . . *No matter how thickly troubled clouds may gather,/* . . . *the Party gives me wisdom and courage*' (Snow, *Stage*: 61, 63). The railway worker

---

[9] Lois Snow finds these villains more interesting as characters than the heroes.

Li Yung-chi also follows '*the Party to drive out those beasts* [the bandits]' (Snow, *Stage*: 77).

The Great Helmsman Mao, to be sure, guides the Communist Party, and he is often acknowledged in *Taking Tiger Mountain by Strategy*. The hero characters state, 'The Communist Party and Chairman Mao will back us up', for the People's Liberation Army is 'dedicated to the Party and Chairman Mao' (Snow, *Stage*: 50). Yang sings, '*The Party's every word is victory's guarantee,/ Mao Tsetung Thought is eternally glorious*'; and Mother Li affirms his sentiment – 'We owe it all to the Communist Party and Chairman Mao' (Snow, *Stage*: 81, 86).

Tiger Mountain is an actual mountain on the mainland, but the opera may suggest the allegory that the tiger shot dead on the mountain and the bandits' stronghold is really the capitalist enemy who will be defeated both directly and by strategy. Typical revolutionary slogans to rally the troops against the villains are contained in the dialogue, such as, 'Be resolute, fear no sacrifice and surmount every difficulty – To win victory' (Snow, *Stage*: 42). The heroes are courageous and clever, using disguise and seeing through traps devised by their enemies. The villains are cowardly and easily duped. They, in the words of Lois Snow, 'are destroyed without a trace of spectator sympathy: the triumph of sheer good over stark evil is mandatory and inevitable. No tears are shed for the vanquished' (*Stage*: 32). Snow, witnessing a production of *Taking Tiger Mountain by Strategy*, reports that when the curtain reopened after the end of the drama, the cast broke into the patriotic song 'Sailing the Seas with the Helmsman'. Soon thereafter, she writes, 'The audience stood and joined in the singing' (*Stage*: 38).

To be sure, Shakespeare was not above writing propagandistic and nationalistic plays. Even in the West many critics see some of his history plays, tragedies, and comedies as variously disguised allegories of the playwright's early modern England. *Julius Caesar*, for example, can be read as anticipating Queen Elizabeth's death and the difficulties associated with a smooth succession; *The Merchant of Venice* may not be about Venice at all but an older,

aristocratic England (Belmont) and a newer, more urban and capitalist England (suggested by Venice).[10]

Shakespeare also was not above writing melodrama. Although
Henry V and *Taking Tiger Mountain* are from radically different
times, genres, and cultural traditions, they nonetheless share
some significant similarities. Both support and defend the established government and promote its version of history. King
Henry, like Yang, is a clear model hero, and although not literally
from the masses is connected to them. Prince Hal frequents
Falstaff's tavern world in the *Henry IV* plays, and the myth that
grew up about his youthful antics associates him with common
folk. In *Henry V*, before the battle of Agincourt, the disguised king
moves among and sympathizes with ordinary soldiers, sharing
their hopes and understanding their fears. He says to Bates,
Court, and Williams, when disguised as Harry le Roy, 'I think the
King is but a man, as I am. The violet smells to him as it doth to
me; the element shows to him as it doth to me; all his senses have
but human conditions. His ceremonies laid by, in his nakedness he
appears but a man' (IV, i, 101–105). Henry's famous St Crispin
speech contains the following lines emphasizing his commonality:
'For he to-day that sheds his blood with me/ Shall be my brother;
be he ne'er so vile,/ This day shall gentle his condition' (IV, iii,
61–63). Just as the bandits in *Tiger Mountain*, the French in *Henry
V* are obvious villains who fight dirty (for example, the retreating
'cowardly rascals' kill the boys guarding the 'luggage'). Before the
battle of Agincourt, the Dauphin and his cohorts, like the *Tiger*
bandits, are shown to be unduly smug and confident of their
prowess. Rhetorical flourishes are common to both dramas, as
is the expected outcome of the climactic battle of the 'good
guys' against overwhelming odds. The appeals to Mao and the
Communist Party can be likened to Henry's prayers to God in
Shakespeare's play.

---

[10] See Murray J. Levith, *Shakespeare's Italian Settings and Plays*, New York:
St. Martin's, 1989: 23.

On the other hand, Shakespeare's play is obviously quite different from this model Chinese opera. While one might argue that Shakespeare's plot is similarly exaggerated melodrama, *Henry V* contains as well a tonal range and complexity of characterization much broader than the opera's. A Chorus sets the scenes, and the characters are distinctive and various. They speak in their own individual ways and some have distinctive dialects – Fluellen, Jamy, and Macmorris, for example. There is comic business in Shakespeare's play. Pistol's encounter with the fearful French soldier is one instance, but there are also the Fluellen scenes with Pistol, Jamy and Macmorris, and, of course, Princess Katherine's bawdy English lesson. *Taking Tiger Mountain by Strategy* exhibits mostly plodding ideological earnestness, while Shakespeare's play provides, among other things, romantic interest with King Henry's wooing of the French princess. Romantic love is, of course, played down in all Chinese model opera: 'If the hero looked for the girl first it would mean his class consciousness is low' (Snow, *Stage*: 208). Next to Shakespeare, *Tiger Mountain*'s characters seem wooden and one-dimensional stereotypes. But the point here is that Shakespeare was not above being nationalistic and patriotic in his plays, in the histories especially. However, the playwright also along the way often raised thoughtful questions about government and leadership, rather than merely reinforcing an ideological status quo. What should be done about a king not cut out for his job? Is regicide justified? What about divine right? Is it proper to seek kingship?

Madame Mao understood, as Edgar Snow reported in *Red Star Over China*, 'There was no more powerful weapon of propaganda in the Communist movement than the Reds' dramatic troupes' (quoted in Snow, *Stage*: 102). Thus, she attacked 'revolutionary actors clothed in velvet and silk presenting Shakespeare . . . for peasants, workers, and soldiers with no background to understand the anomaly' (Snow, *Stage*: 15). She insisted that criticism, in turn, discuss a given work of art 'in terms of its meaning for the masses and not in terms of its purely cultural or aesthetic role' (Snow, *Stage*: 104). She wished to develop a new and purely socialist, national culture. The Red Army used the theatre for educational purposes, and Jiang Qing not only continued this practice, but expanded it during the Cultural Revolution.

* * *

Following the 1989 Tiananmen Square massacre, Lois Wheeler Snow had a change of heart about PRC government policy that she supported so innocently and ardently in the seventies. In a *Time Magazine* interview she acknowledged, 'Tiananmen just woke me up' ('Interview', 11 June 2001). Returning to the PRC after an absence of more than a decade, around the time of the 2001 Tiananmen anniversary in June, she wished to meet with Professor Ding Zilin, a dissident whose son was killed during the democracy demonstrations. She was prevented from doing so by the authorities, a leadership Snow accuses of withholding monies collected abroad for the families of massacre victims. Mrs Snow's response was to threaten to remove her husband's ashes from his Beijing University burial site. Edgar Snow's headstone there reads in both Chinese and English: 'Edgar Snow, American Friend of the Chinese People'. But while Mrs Snow's recent public statements about human rights in China suggest recognition of the PRC's political repression, her 1972 book casts a blind eye to massive human rights violations and repression during a much harsher, earlier time of terror. It was indeed then, in Shakespeare's words from *Titus Andronicus*, 'a wilderness of tigers' (III, i, 54).

Miranda, too, casts an innocent eye on the characters she sees near the end of Shakespeare's *The Tempest*, but we know not all of them are 'good'. The world is not uniformly splendid, 'brave'. Thus, Prospero tempers his daughter's exclamation with these words of experience, 'It's new to thee' (V, i, 184). He knows of the plots, the desire for power, how power corrupts and can be cruelly employed. But Prospero also forgives.

CHAPTER FOUR

After the Cultural Revolution, 1976–2000

'A local habitation . . .' (*A Midsummer Night's Dream*, V, i, 17)

'It is said that within hours of the death of Mao', J. Philip Brockbank writes, 'queues formed in the streets for copies of Shakespeare's most popular play in China, *The Pound of Flesh* [*The Merchant of Venice*]'.[1] However, Shakespeare on the mainland has had several setbacks as well as successes since 1976. Deng Xiaoping's 'Socialism with Chinese characteristics' and his 'open door' policy included more engagement with the West, but there were also official anti-foreign episodes along the way – for example, in the wake of the 1989 Tiananmen 'incident'.

The most significant event for the revitalization of Shakespeare activity after the Cultural Revolution was the long-delayed 1978 publication of Zhu Shenghao's translation of Shakespeare, as supplemented and edited by various scholars to yield a *Complete Works of Shakespeare* [*Shashibiya quanji*]. Although somewhat expurgated, this edition represents the first translated complete works of any foreign author to be published in the PRC. Initially scheduled to appear in 1964 to commemorate the 400th anniversary of

---

[1] 'Shakespeare Renaissance in China', *Shakespeare Quarterly* 39: 2 (Summer 1988): 197.

Shakespeare's birth, publication was cancelled as Cultural Revolution clouds loomed on the horizon. When Zhu's edition finally did appear, there soon followed a number of other fresh translations and reissues of older translations. Fang Ping's *Five Comedies by Shakespeare* [*Shashibiya xiju wuzhong*] sees print in 1979, and includes *A Midsummer Night's Dream*, *The Merchant of Venice*, *Much Ado About Nothing*, *The Merry Wives of Windsor*, and *The Tempest*.[2] Cao Weifeng's four tragedies – *Romeo and Juliet*, *Hamlet*, *Othello*, *Macbeth* – was also reissued, as was a ninth printing of Cao Yu's *Romeo and Juliet*. Lin Tongji's new translation of *Hamlet* [*Danmai wangzi Hamulei de beiju*], which had taken him more than twenty years to accomplish, was in press in 1983, and Tu An's rendering of the sonnets received numerous printings during the eighties. Additionally, in 1988 Bian Zhilin published verse translations of the four great tragedies [*Shashibiya beiju sizhong*] – *Hamlet*, *Othello*, *King Lear*, and *Macbeth* – the last three of which were new translations.

Mainland Shakespeare in the World

This period not only saw a focus on translation, and generally rising interest in Shakespeare by the educated public, but it also witnessed a number of events that signalled the Chinese mainland's re-entry into the world of global Shakespeare activity. In 1980 dramatist Cao Yu, whose own plays show Shakespeare's influence, together with Zhao Xun, Wu Shiliang, and Ying Ruocheng, visited Stratford-upon-Avon to present Zhu Shenghao's *Complete Works* to the Royal Shakespeare Company there. The first of the eleven volumes is inscribed from 'the Chinese Dramatists' Association', and the set is now housed in the Shakespeare Centre library. Marking the occasion, actor Ying Ruocheng offered a

---

[2] The translator presented this volume to the Shakespeare Centre, Stratford-upon-Avon, in 1982.

reading of a number of Shakespeare sonnets in Chinese.[3] Also in Stratford in the eighties, academics from the PRC attended various international Shakespeare conferences. Fudan University Professor Lu Gusun was among them, and his paper 'Hamlet Across Space and Time' subsequently appeared in print in *Shakespeare Survey 36*.[4] In it Lu reviews the history of *Hamlet* in China, emphasizing its affinities with Chinese drama to explain its appeal, and then focuses on 'the "relationships" approach' and Hamlet's 'inability to identify' in the context of the play. Lu concludes: 'only relationships – various and ubiquitous in a modern man's milieu – remain agelessly and universally real.'

An exhibition entitled 'Shakespeare's Time' was organized in Beijing in 1981, and *The Shakespeare Quarterly* bibliography began noting Chinese Shakespeare studies for the first time in 1985. Another significant milestone was the reading of Qiu Ke'an's paper at the Third World Shakespeare Congress in West Berlin (1986), attended by Professors Chang Junchuan and Suo Tianzhang. Active participation by Chinese scholars at subsequent international conferences followed, and today China sends its Shakespeareans to meetings all over the world.

Although a few Shakespeare groups had been formed in the early eighties, 1984 marks the official founding of The Shakespeare Society of China [*Zhongguo Shashibiya yanjiuhui*], with subsequent membership in the International Shakespeare Association. Hu Qiaomu, then Honorary President of the Society (and Secretary of the Chinese Communist Party), blessed the new organization with the following, somewhat curious message: 'The work of the members of the Shakespeare Society of China will surely result in broader and deeper understanding, sympathy, and respect for our nation's social and cultural development' (quoted in Meng, *Survey*: 39). This fledgling but ambitious group of scholars and theatre

---

[3] See article on Ying Ruocheng by Patricia Wilson, '. . . A Real Interpreter Who Can Act', *Chinese Literature* 3 (March 1982): 55–72.

[4] Ed. Stanley Wells, Cambridge: Cambridge University Press, 1983: 53–56.

people soon planned a Shakespeare Festival, and organized the publication of Shakespeare's plays in bilingual annotated editions. In December, 1984, Qiu Ke'an's *Hamlet* appeared as the initial volume in the series, and its editor explained that with increasing numbers of Chinese able to read Shakespeare in English many early-modern allusions, words, and ideas needed to be discussed to bridge cultural and historical gaps. The series is not yet complete, and volumes continue to be added to this day.[5]

Shakespeare Studies [*Shashibiya yanjiu*], launched in 1983, became the Society's responsibility, and it represents the very first scholarly journal on the mainland devoted to a non-Chinese writer. In his 'Inaugural Observations' to introduce the journal, Cao Yu, first president of the Society, articulates its dual purpose:

> to publish critical essays on Shakespeare and also articles concerning the playwright on the Chinese stage. Our aim is to recognize Shakespeare as a great Elizabethan [*sic*] dramatist and poet whose plays require both literary and theatrical research and study. If literary scholars cooperate closely and

---

[5] Qiu Ke'an, 'Annotated *Hamlet* Available', *China Daily*, 5 February 1985: 5, 6. In addition to Qiu's Second Edition of *Hamlet* with revised notes (2001), the following plays have been published by the Commercial Press in Beijing: *Julius Caesar* (ed. Qiu Ke'an, 1985), *A Midsummer Night's Dream* (ed. Qiu Ke'an, 1987), *Twelfth Night* (ed. Zhi Jingzhong, 1987), *Much Ado About Nothing* (ed. Shen Enrong, 1987), *Henry V* (ed. Zhi Jingzhong, 1987), *The Merchant of Venice* (ed. Zhang Wenting, 1989), *Henry IV, Part 1* (ed. Zhang Wenting, 1989), *Romeo and Juliet* (ed. Gu Jingyu, 1990), *The Sonnets* (ed. Qian Zhaoming, 1990), *The Winter's Tale* (ed. Du Shao, 1990), *As You Like It* (eds. Luo Zhiye and Li Derong, 1990), *Measure for Measure* (ed. Zhang Xinwei, 1990), *The Tempest* (ed. Shen Enrong, 1990), *Macbeth* (ed. Qiu Ke'an, 1992), *Troilus and Cressida* (ed. He Qixin, 1995), *Antony and Cleopatra* (ed. Qiu Ke'an, 1995), *The Comedy of Errors* (ed. Zhi Jingzhong, 1995), *Richard III* (ed. Yang Lingui, 1997), *Othello* (ed. Shen Enrong, 2001), *King Lear* (ed. Zhang Xinwei, 2001), *King John* (ed. Zhi Jingzhong, 2001), *The Two Noble Kinsmen* (ed. Sun Fali, 2001), *Henry VIII* (ed. Zhi Jingzhong, 2001), *The Taming of the Shrew* (eds. Luo Zhiye and Luo Yisha, 2002), and *Love's Labour's Lost* (ed. Yin Yao, 2002).

Figure 1. Professor Qiu Ke'an holding one of his Shakespeare editions.

harmoniously with those who act Shakespeare, I believe we can advance both critical studies and improve stage productions.[6]

Cao goes on to stress, 'we are reading the world giant Shakespeare from the point of view of a modern China involved in its own recent history'. Thus, he continues, 'We attempt to study Shakespeare from a Marxist perspective'. But Cao also suggests that Chinese scholars should 'approach Shakespeare's great soul from many different angles'. He believes that the playwright can 'enrich Chinese culture; . . . Shakespeare broadens our field of vision and causes us to appreciate the finer things in life while eschewing the baser. Shakespeare work is vast, and studying him teaches us that there seem as many shining poems and interesting characters as there are stars in the sky.' Although the journal *Shakespeare Studies* has appeared somewhat erratically over the years since its first publication, it nonetheless continues to be a primary outlet for Chinese Shakespeare scholarship and criticism.

In addition to the national society, provincial Shakespeare societies were also founded beginning in the mid-eighties. The first of these was the Shakespeare Society of Jilin Province in 1985, whose familiar patriotic goal is 'implementing the policy of "letting a hundred flowers bloom and a hundred schools of thought contend," and working arduously for Shakespeare studies from a recognizably Chinese perspective' (quoted in Meng, *Survey*: 39). Other Shakespeare societies followed, including ones in Zhejiang Province and in the cities of Tianjin, Wuhan, and Hangzhou.

Also in the early eighties, Professor Lin Tongji established a Shakespeare research library at Shanghai's Fudan University, and in 1984 Beijing's Central Academy of Drama created a 'Shakespeare Research Centre'. Both are important repositories of Shakespeare materials for study, although now other universities and drama schools also collect Shakespeare materials. For

---

[6] Cao Yu, 'Inaugural observations', *Shakespeare Studies* (China) 1: 1–4; this essay was reprinted from the *People's Daily* [*Renmin ribao*] (5 April 1983) where it was titled *Xiang Shashibiya xuexi* ['Learn From Shakespeare'].

example, Northeast Normal University in Changchun, which established its own Shakespeare Research Centre in 1994.

Productions

As might be expected, Shanghai and Beijing have been the major venues for staging Shakespeare during the last two decades of the twentieth century. After the enforced censorship of the Cultural Revolution, the flurry of important modern productions began in 1979 with the Shanghai Youth Theatre's *Much Ado About Nothing* [*Wushi shengfei*].[7] Also in 1979, both in Shanghai and Beijing, Derek Jacobi and the Old Vic gave nine performances of *Hamlet* in English (with earphone translation available to audiences). This production, part of a world tour sponsored by the British Council, was the first appearance by a British company on mainland stages since the founding of the People's Republic. The last night of the tour included a televised performance that reached an estimated audience of ten million viewers, according to London's *Evening Standard* (11 June 1979). Commenting on this *Hamlet* production, Fox Butterfield, *The New York Times* Beijing bureau chief at the time, writes: 'The Chinese audiences were clearly unprepared for . . . [Derek Jacobi's] exuberant, almost uninhibited style of acting, which is far more naturalistic than that permitted to Chinese actors by their theatrical canon' (25 November 1979). Butterfield continues, the audiences judged as 'insufficiently royal for Chinese taste' Brenda Bruce's portrayal of Gertrude with 'hoarse voice and bounteous cleavage'.

At least four Shakespeare plays were staged in 1980. Perhaps the most important of these was *The Merchant of Venice*, the first *Merchant* in almost twenty years and the first Shakespeare to be

---

[7] See Wilkinson, 'Shakespeare': 50. Li Ruru overlooks this production when she writes, 'The first Shakespeare performance [*The Merchant of Venice*] in the post-Cultural Revolution era took place in Beijing in 1980' ('Bard': 65).

acted by the influential Beijing Chinese Youth Art Theatre. According to Li Ruru, this production marked 'a revival of literature and art in China after the Cultural Revolution' ('Bard': 65). Directed by Zhang Qihong, with Cao Yu acting as artistic advisor, *Merchant* was performed in various cities more than two hundred times between 1980–1982, shown often on television, and revived for the 1986 Chinese Shakespeare Festival. It also won several awards from the Ministry of Culture (Fan, 'Shakespeare': 29).[8] The production broke from past theatrical modesty, as it contained on-stage kissing and retained Shakespeare's more suggestive lines. Indeed, some, including Fang Ping, were made uncomfortable by the production's exhibitionism and frankness, and argued that it was vulgar and morally offensive to Chinese tastes. However Zhang Qihong, the Moscow-trained director, downplayed such criticism. She informed the inaugural meeting of The Shakespeare Society of China that her aim was not to offend common sensibilities, but rather 'to explore and display Shakespeare's "profound critique of feudalism" and [display the playwright's] "great realism, humanism, and moral power"' in her production (quoted in Fan, 'Shakespeare': 30). To accomplish this, she cut the roughly twenty-or-so scenes in the original play down to twelve, and eliminated most of the references to the religious conflict between Shylock and the Christians. In Act I, for example, Shylock's lines referring to Antonio, 'I hate him for he is a Christian:/ But more, for that in low simplicity/ He lends out money gratis' (iii, 42–44), become, 'I hate him for that in low simplicity/ He lends out money gratis' (quoted in Li, 'Bard': 66). Similarly, in Act III, scene i, Zhang substituted the word 'money-lender' for 'Jew'. Zhang asks, 'Wasn't it better for us simply to reduce the *unessential* [italics mine] points made in the play . . .?' (Li, 'Bard': 67). Most would argue, however, that the religious theme in *Merchant* is most essential and crucial to its meaning. Zhang's justification was that Chinese audiences would not be interested in the Jewish and Christian conflict, that Shylock is

---

[8] See also He Qixin's comments on the production in *STCE*: 154–57.

most importantly a 'feudal usurer' and Antonio a 'rising capital-ist', and that Shakespeare's play is centrally about 'generosity, honesty, friendship, and love' (Fan, 'Shakespeare': 30). Thus, Zhang played her Shylock as mostly a melodramatic and selfish villain. She even viewed the Duke's pardon of Shylock as 'a tender mercy', and left out Shakespeare's cruel twist-of-the-knife conver-sion at the end of the play (Li, 'Bard': 66). Wigs, artificial noses, and make-up were employed to make the Asian actors look West-ern. On the other side, stylized dancing in the casket scene made use of a Chinese theatrical convention. Although this production did spark controversy, it also prompted fruitful discussion about *The Merchant of Venice*, Shakespeare, and drama in general that came as a relief after the repression of the Cultural Revolution.

In 1981 Ying Ruocheng, the same actor who read sonnets in Stratford-upon-Avon, translated and co-directed a *Measure for Measure* together with Toby Robertson, director of the Jacobi *Hamlet* seen two years earlier. At first glance, Shakespeare's tragic-comic problem play seems a rather odd choice for a joint-venture project, with its religious dimension, clear social class divisions, and criminal underworld. But, as Stephen Greenblatt astutely observes, 'its plot concerns the enigmatic withdrawal from author-ity of the rightful duke, and the rise and fall of a fanatical, self-righteous, and corrupt lieutenant – in short one version of recent Chinese history [read, the period of the Cultural Revolution]'.[9] Angelo's severe 'new' order, suggesting the rule of Jiang Qing and the Gang of Four, is contrasted with the Duke's merciful 'old' order of relaxed law enforcement. Angelo is 're-educated' and repentant in the end, a lesson for those who strayed. Even more to the play's point is the lesson about the impotence of 'truth' in the face of abused power, clearly reminiscent of China's recent past. Additionally, there is the theme of forgiveness. Shake-speare's *Measure for Measure*, according to Chinese interpretation, also critiques the morality and seamy side of early modern England. That is, the playwright attacks moral, religious, and

---

[9] 'China: Visiting Rites', *Raritan* 2:4 (1983): 19.

political hypocrisy, self-interest, feudalism, and corruption in high places.

For this production, *Measure for Measure*'s title was changed to *Please Step into the Furnace*, alluding to a familiar Tang Dynasty story about a corrupt official. The play script was severely altered as well. For example, allusions to God, prostitution, and political ideas contrary to PRC ideology, some five hundred lines, were excised from the text (He, *STCE*: 23, n.38; 157–58). On the other hand, reminders of Cultural Revolution humiliations were added. Claudio and Julietta appeared wearing white dunce caps; rhythmic drumbeats and cacophonous noise accompanied their early entrances, reminiscent of Red Guard harassment. The actors were allowed to look Asian; that is, not made up to look Western. Carolyn Wakeman's review in the *Shakespeare Quarterly* is lavish in its praise. Wakeman writes, 'Shakespeare's play achieved a level of excellence worthy of admiration of emulation anywhere in the world.' She was especially impressed with Ying Ruocheng's translation: it 'captured with astonishing effectiveness, in the idiom of the Peking streets, the pungency and bawdiness of Shakespeare's punning humor, while transmitting with equal deftness the stately eloquence and dignified formality of the courtly characters' speech'.[10]

Also in 1981, the Shanghai Drama Institute's first graduating class of Tibetan students produced a *Romeo and Juliet* in both Tibetan and Chinese, which initially played in Shanghai and Beijing. The following year it was staged in Lhasa. Director Xu Qiping reports,

rehearsals were an eye-opener. In many ways they [the Tibetan actors] did better than Han students. In expressing love Han students were more reserved. Tibetan students, on the other hand, were more spontaneous, more straight forward. The girls embraced passionately. The men fought the duels fiercely,

---

[10] '*Measure for Measure*, On the Chinese Stage', *Shakespeare Quarterly* 33:4 (Winter 1982): 499, 502.

breaking eleven swords during the rehearsals. All in all, they threw themselves into the performance with a youthful ardor.[11]

Although this production was clearly a milestone for minority Shakespeare in China, He Qixin questions the insertion of non-Shakespearean Mandarin lines, at times apparently merely to elicit audience laughter (He, *STCE*: 159–60).[12]

1982 saw The British Council's English offering of a reduced cast *Twelfth Night*, directed by John Fraser, which toured to Beijing, Nanjing, and Shanghai. In the same year, British actress Tsai Chin (also known as Zhou Caiqin) directed *The Tempest*. The Chinese Ministry of Culture had invited Chin to the Central Academy of Drama to be its first 'foreign expert', and she details her experience in an informative essay.[13] Tsai notes her reasons for choosing Shakespeare's romance over other possibilities:

> The play has similarities with many Beijing operas and provided me an opportunity to experiment with synthesizing the two forms. Tragic and comic scenes juxtapose in the play's structure. Miranda and Ferdinand conform to the Chinese ideals of love and marriage: purity, chastity, and parental consent with celestial blessing. A Chinese audience could also easily identify with this story of calamity, injustice, and revenge. Moreover, the theme of the play was especially topical, concerning as it does a lesson in forgiveness, which mirrored the attitude adopted by the Chinese people towards their former persecutors during the Cultural Revolution.

---

[11] Quoted in Wang Zuoliang, ed., *Preliminary Essays on Shakespeare – and Shakespeare in China*, Chongqing: Chongqing chubanshe, 1991: 212–13.

[12] The Central Academy of Drama later mounted two Mongolian minority productions, *Othello* and *A Midsummer Night's Dream*, in 1986.

[13] Tsai was the daughter of Beijing opera actor Zhou Xinfang, who died during the Cultural Revolution. See article by Tsai Chin, 'Teaching and Directing in China: Chinese Theatre Revisited', *Asian Theatre Journal* 3:1 (1986): 118–31.

Tsai goes on to discuss details of *The Tempest* production itself:
> The set consisted of only two rocks, so that the students did not
> have to compete with the elaborate sets which the Chinese are
> so good at painting. The costumes were basic tunics and trou-
> sers not identified with any particular period or country. . . .
> Miranda, the only mortal woman in the play, wore a long dress.
> Symbolic colors were used to denote status and character, a
> notion borrowed from Beijing opera. The spirits wore stylized
> make-up, as did Trinculo and Stephano, who wore a combin-
> ation of Chinese and Western clown make-up. . . . Prospero
> was to be a relatively young man.

Her Caliban was not played as the monstrous creature he is usu-
ally imagined to be, but rather as a more sympathetic victim of
Prospero's colonialism. At the end of the play he stands proudly
on the very rock that the duke mounted at the start of the action.
According to one critic, Chin's production skilfully combined
Chinese spirit with Shakespeare's intention.[14]

The years 1983 to 1986 featured a *Romeo and Juliet* ballet and
productions of mostly tragedies, including a 1985 *King Lear*, the
first *Lear* to be staged in the PRC. Among the several Chinese
opera adaptations was Shao Hongchao's experimental 1983
Othello [*Aosailuo*], a version that won praise from Cao Yu. For this
opera adaptation, Shakespeare's plot was compressed to a prologue and seven scenes (Wilkinson, 'Shakespeare': 53–54).[15]
Replacing Shakespeare's opening dialogue was a special soliloquy
written for Othello, intended to introduce the tragic hero to the
audience, and delivered in a St. Mark's Square setting. Other
significant alterations included Othello falling in love with

---

[14] Quoted in Tsai Chin, 'Teaching and Directing in China: Chinese
Theatre Revisited', *Asian Theatre Journal* 3:1 (1986): 124.
[15] See discussion of this production in Geremie Barme, 'Not Wisely
But Too Well—*Othello* in Beijing', *Chinese Literature* (September 1983):
114–18; also, Zhang Xiaoyang, *Shakespeare*: 146–50.

Figure 2. Othello [Aosailuo] 1986; revival of 1983 production.

Desdemona at first sight, and Iago's clearly stated, unambiguous motivation. Iago declares,

> I am not a villain. The black general himself has entailed all the evil consequences: he did not appoint me as his lieutenant; there is [no] doubt that he has had an affair with my wife; I also love Desdemona, but he got her before I had a chance to. My hellish hatred against him has led me to a bitter revenge . . . I'll call on the god of vengeance to lend me a hand (quoted in He, *STCE*: 163–64).

As for Desdemona, in the words of an Australian critic, she was turned 'into a flippant and even coquettish tart' (Barme, '*Othello*': 117). While this *Othello* upset Chinese opera lovers and Shakespeare purists alike, both of whom objected to the mixing of genres and 'the sheer outlandishness of Shakespeare in Chinese', the opera's cultural fusion led to energetic discussion among theatre people. Of course, the question for Shakespeareans was: when is what purports to be Shakespeare not really Shakespeare at all? That is to say, when is Shakespeare a *source* or *inspiration* rather than an interpretation? How far can an adaptation go before it no longer has a legitimate connection with a given Shakespeare play? Is Otto Nicolai's *The Merry Wives of Windsor*, or Verdi's *Macbeth*, *Otello*, or *Falstaff* in fact Shakespeare? We recall Lord Byron's comment about Gioacchino Rossini's *Otello*: 'They have been crucifying Othello into an opera . . . Music good but lugubrious – but as for the words!'[16] Is *Kiss Me Kate* or *West Side Story* still Shakespeare? How about *Rosencrantz and Guildenstern Are Dead*? Or the films *Throne of Blood, Ran, My Own Private Idaho*, and *Ten Things I Hate About You*? Prokofiev's or Tschaikovsky's *Romeo and Juliet* ballets? Is a genre shift or plot summary by the Lambs still Shakespeare? Or, for that matter, even a scholarly translation into Chinese of a folio text of *Macbeth*? Any contemporary theatre *production* in English surely *interprets* a given text, and often modern-

---

[16] '*The Flesh is Frail': Byron's Letters and Journals 6 (1818–19)*, ed. Leslie A. Marchand, Cambridge, MA: Harvard University Press, 1976: 18.

izes or changes the setting, perhaps adds materials and/or makes cuts and structural rearrangements, but the result still seems 'Shakespeare'. On the other hand, can a streamlined or altered plot, opera adaptation in Chinese – names and title changed, opera conventions honoured – still be considered authentic Shakespeare, or is Shakespeare's plot merely a launch pad for something else? The answer to this question goes to the heart of most of what the Chinese call 'Shakespeare'.

The 1986 Shakespeare Festival

The productions following the Cultural Revolution led up to China's first Shakespeare Festival, which was organized by The Shakespeare Society of China, the Chinese Dramatic Art Research Society, and the Beijing and Shanghai Drama Academies. It took place from 10 to 23 April 1986, and during this time more than two dozen versions of sixteen Shakespeare plays appeared in various formats on PRC stages.[17] Some of them were revivals of popular earlier productions, such as Zhang Qihong's *The Merchant of Venice* and the Beijing Opera *Othello*. Four were Chinese premieres – *Titus Andronicus*, *Richard III*, *Love's Labour's Lost*, and *The Merry Wives of Windsor*; six were adaptations in various styles and permutations; and one was a puppet play (Li, 'Bard':

---

[17] The numbers of productions and plays vary with the reporters. Li Ruru writes, 'At the festival twenty-seven drama companies, drama and theatre academies, universities, and studios presented sixteen plays in twenty-eight produtions' ('Bard': 69); J. Philip Brockbank agrees: 'twenty-eight productions, of which twelve were in Beijing and sixteen in Shanghai; . . . some two dozen companies at a dozen theatres performed eighteen different plays' ('Renaissance': 196). But J. Norman Wilkinson writes, 'Beijing produced 11 plays in 12 days, while Shanghai staged 14 plays in 14 days' ('Shakespeare': 51). Yang Henghesng, in *China Today*, has 'Twenty-five versions of 15 plays' (35:7 [July 1986]: 41).

Figure 3. Nerissa and Portia, *The Merchant of Venice* 1986; revival of
1980 production.

70).[18] Lectures, seminars, and book publications supplemented the stage presentations. Some of the Festival's offerings were university or amateur efforts, but others were by professional theatre and opera troupes. The People's Liberation Army Art Theatre's *The Merchant of Venice* and Beijing's Second Foreign Language Institute's *Timon of Athens* were the only two given in English. A reported audience of over 100,000 people attended some seventy live performances, yet so popular was the Festival that several productions were nationally televised to reach the widest possible audience (Yang, *China*: 41). One such was the Shanghai Youth Art Theatre's *Antony and Cleopatra*. This production forwarded a traditional version of the tragedy that included costumes suggesting Rome and Egypt, and a simple set consisting of multipurpose platforms. Also televised was Sun Jiaxiu's adaptation of *King Lear* [*Li Ya Wang*], one of the most notable offerings of the Festival.

Sun, the founder and late Director of the Central Academy of Drama's Shakespeare Research Centre (established in 1984), offered a detailed account of her *King Lear* script and stage production in a 1988 article.[19] Noting the nearly 'impossible' task of 'following Shakespeare closely and not tampering with anything unless out of utter necessity, while at the same time making the play as truly Chinese as it could be', her aim was 'to make our Chinese people not just know of Shakespeare as a great Western playwright, but come to enjoy his plays and feel them relevant to their lives' (Sun, '*King*': 74–75). In programme notes Sun writes, 'By using Chinese characters, language and background, we could shorten, or even remove, the distance between Shakespeare and our people.' Hence, she offered a prose *King Lear* that was a 'hybrid' Shakespeare, an 'artistic fusion of the Oriental and the

---

[18] The opera adaptations included *Much Ado About Nothing*, *Twelfth Night*, *Othello*, *King Lear*, *Macbeth*, and *The Winter's Tale*; the puppet play was *Twelfth Night*.

[19] 'Our Chinese *King Lear–Li Ya Wang*', *Wen Yuan* 3, *Studies in Language, Literature and Culture*, ed. Wang Zuoliang, Beijing: Foreign Language Teaching and Research Press, 1991: 74–81.

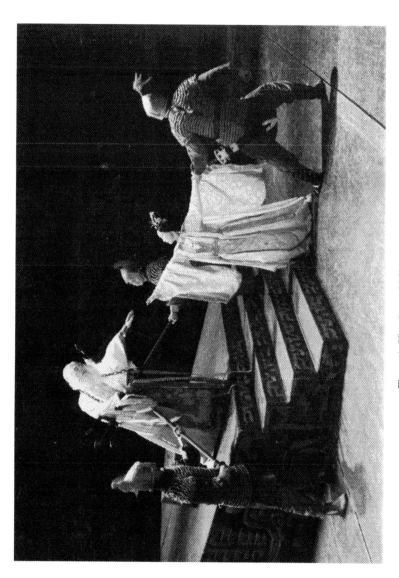

Figure 4. King Lear [Li Yā Wang] 1986.

Western; the traditional and the modern'. She set the tragedy during the Warring States Period, and it featured Chinese costumes, stylized gestures, and opera-style music. Characters were given Chinese names – Li Qing for Cordelia, Ge Hong for Edgar, Ge Mong for Edmund, Zhao Kangzi for Kent. However, rather than acting stock Chinese drama stereotypes, Sun's actors attempted to convey each character's individual psychology. On the thematic level, the focus was 'spotlighting the cruelty of the conflicts between the old and new and between the good and evil during social mutations' (Sun, '*King*': 76–77). In the storm scene, Sun writes, 'We strove to present . . . the powerful momentum of the inner tempests and the profound connotations concerning Man, Nature and Society' ('*King*': 79). This *Li Ya Wang* seemed to many a successful experiment in fusing Shakespeare both with *huaju* and traditional opera styles, and it was considered a great Festival success (see Brockbank, 'Renaissance': 200–201).

Just as with Sun Jiaxiu's *King Lear*, many other Festival offerings were adapted to familiar Chinese opera forms and stage techniques, again raising the question of whether or not such versions were really 'Shakespeare' or something merely inspired by Shakespeare. For instance, there were several opera *Othello*s, one a revival of the 1983 production by the Beijing Experimental Drama Troupe and another by a Shanghai company. Philip Brockbank suggests carefully that the Beijing opera revival 'recreated *Othello* in a convincingly Shakespearean *Chinese* tradition [italics mine]', and notes that racial conflict was played down but class and gender issues were brought to the fore ('Renaissance': 201). The other Chinese opera presentations included *Macbeth, The Winter's Tale, Much Ado About Nothing,* and *Twelfth Night.*

Macbeth became *Bloody Hands* in a *kunju* opera version, performed by the Shanghai Opera Troupe. Directed by Li Jiayao, with Huang Zuolin acting as artistic advisor, this production subsequently travelled to the 1987 Edinburgh Festival, and later toured other cities in the UK. *Kunju*, thought to be the oldest form of Chinese opera and the source for most other Chinese theatre styles, was popular in Shakespeare's own sixteenth century, and is

Figure 5. Professor Sun Jiaxiu with the Author.

the forerunner of both Beijing and *shaoxing* opera.[20] *Bloody Hands* represented a condensed and altered version of *Macbeth* rearranged into eight scenes, with a Chinese setting, singing, dancing, martial arts, stylized gestures, and musical accompaniment.[21] Lady Macbeth, renamed *Tie Shi* for 'Iron Lady', was the clear villain of the piece (much as in Akira Kurosawa's *Throne of Blood*), and she goads her husband into doing his evil deeds, performing some of her own as well. She, and not Macbeth, is the one to plot the murder of 'Banquo' and his son, and she also kills her own younger sister, the 'Lady Macduff' of the opera. *Bloody Hands* adds a squawking parrot-ghost to the plot, which bizarre spirit is intended to emphasize the cruelty of Lady Macbeth.[22] It accuses her of Duncan's murder – parrots being gossips in Chinese mythology (Zha and Tian, 'Shakespeare': 206). *Bloody Hands* replaced the atmospheric dark-night setting of Shakespeare's tragedy with the bright stage spotlight convention of *kunju*, and Shakespeare's renamed characters were amalgamated with *kunju* (and other) opera types. These included the *dan* (woman), with traditional make-up of pink cheeks and eyelids, and the *mo* (middle-aged man). Although Li Ruru considers *Bloody Hands* 'fully sinicized' (see Li, 'Theatre': 38–39), director Li Jiayao insisted that he wished to catch the spirit of the original play and, further, forward 'Shakespeare's humanistic ideal' (Zha and Tian, 'Shakespeare': 205).

An adaptation of *Much Ado About Nothing* employed the opera style associated with Anhui Province. Just as with *Bloody Hands* Chinese names were substituted for Shakespeare's originals, and costumes were meant to recall an ancient China. This time, however, the

---

[20] Zha Peide and Tian Jia, 'Shakespeare and Traditional Chinese Operas', *Shakespeare Quarterly* 39: 2 (Summer 1988): 205.

[21] Li Ruru's entire essay, 'Macbeth Becomes Ma Pei: An Odyssey from Scotland to China', contains 9 detailed description of the opera (*Theatre Research International* 20: 1 [1995]: 42–53).

[22] Li Ruru, 'Chinese Traditional Theatre and Shakespeare', *Asian Theatre Journal* 5:1 (Spring 1988): 39.

production closely followed Shakespeare's original plot, characterization, and sequence of scenes (Li, 'Theatre': 40). The setting
was in an unspecified minority locale during a vague antique
dynasty, in order to make credible the invective and wit of
Shakespeare's dialogue that would not accord with modest Han
practice (Fei, *Theories*: 189). Zha Peide and Tian Jia write that this
Much Ado About Nothing opera retained 'much of the play's original
poetic quality' ('Shakespeare': 208), but their precise meaning is
unclear. Shakespeare's comedy, of course, is written mostly in prose.

The Winter's Tale and *Twelfth Night* were done in the *shaoxing*
opera style, associated with Zhejiang Province. Reversing
Shakespeare's early modern practice (and some Chinese opera
conventions), an all-woman cast presented an abridged and 'sina-
cized' *The Winter's Tale*. Autolycus' songs, for example, became
rhythmic chanting to drum accompaniment, typical of *shaoxing*
opera (Brockbank, 'Renaissance': 202). On the other hand, Hu
Weimin's opera *Twelfth Night* attempted to retain some 'foreign'
flavour. The setting remained Shakespeare's Illyria, original character names were retained, and the costumes were obviously foreign (Zha and Tian, 'Shakespeare': 210). However, some of the
arias and music, foot and hand gestures, and swordplay combined
shaoxing opera and Western features. Director Hu wanted his production to 'definitely possess the distinctive cultural and artistic
characteristics unique to this regional (*shaoxing*) theatre form in
Shanghai, China [but adds, speaking to his actors], the central
focus should be on Shakespeare, on making every effort to convey
the essence of his work faithfully' (Fei, *Theories*: 190). The key
word, of course, is 'essence', for again we have Shakespeare trans-
ferred to another genre as an inspiration or 'source'.

Other Festival productions included The China Coal Miners'
Troupe's *A Midsummer Night's Dream*, which employed electronic
music, green lights for forest effects, and a Bottom 'transformed'
with a Beijing Opera mask. Oberon and Titania's quarrel was
over an eight-function digital watch, prized in the PRC in the mid-
eighties, as opposed to a changeling boy! Philip Brockbank
attended a Children's Art Theatre *Richard III*, the first history

Figure 6. A Midsummer Night's Dream 1986.

play to be staged in China (Brockbank, 'Renaissance': 198–200; 196–97). Of this production he writes guardedly, it 'was less disorienting than it might have been, and more commendable for what it seemed to conserve from a familiar tradition than for its Chinese initiatives'.

In his comprehensive essay 'Reflections After the Curtainfall', Fudan University Professor Lu Gusun poses the question: what next for Shakespeare activity in China?[23] He suggests that scholars should focus on the playwright's themes, symbolism, and representation of truth. Theatre people, he believes, should be encouraged to stage plays and also cautiously experiment with adapting them to traditional Chinese opera styles. Because Shakespeare's poetic language is often difficult even in translation, 'we will guide the audience to understand Shakespeare's themes rather than his style'. Throwing in the necessary political bromide, Lu says the playwright is helpful not only for China's cultural life, but also for her 'socialist construction'. After all, he reminds us, Shakespeare praises truth, beauty, kindness, and human feeling, while criticizing feudalism, superstition, and religion.

Following the Festival, The Shakespeare Society of China published a volume of twelve essays, some of which were written especially for the book. Additionally, the journal *Theatre Arts* [*Xiju yishu*] printed a dialogue between Hu Weimin and Ye Changhai on the subject of the integration of Shakespeare with traditional Chinese theatre. Thus, the first Chinese Shakespeare Festival was not only an important milestone for Shakespeare production in China, but it also served to raise relevant scholarly and critical issues about Shakespeare, adaptation, and the playwright's overall role in the PRC.

---

[23] *Shakespeare Studies (China)* 1:18–42.

Figure 7. Richard III 1986.

1993 Wuhan Conference

The 1993 Wuhan International Shakespeare Conference, sponsored by Wuhan University, offered forty papers, mostly on the topics Shakespeare's humanism, imagery, and the playwright in a comparative context.[24] Shakespeare scholars from around the PRC were joined by several academics from the US and Hong Kong. Important older Chinese Shakespeareans, such as Fang Ping, participated in the conference, and younger scholars read papers reflecting both Chinese approaches and newer approaches familiar in the West. For example, Wang Lili's essay about the 'Female Characters in *Hamlet*' was a feminist reading comparing Gertrude and Ophelia with other women characters in the tragedies. Another paper attempted to connect Shakespeare with *qigong* – the traditional Chinese internal energy discipline! For entertainment, students from Wuhan University, under the direction of Professor David Perry, performed scenes in English from *A Midsummer Night's Dream* and *As You Like It*, and a group from Central China Normal University offered *Othello*. A special feature of the conference was the introduction of Sun Fali's translation of *The Two Noble Kinsmen*, the first Chinese rendering of this play. Sun's remarks considered authorship problems in *The Two Noble Kinsmen*, its inclusion in the Shakespeare canon, and other relevant issues connected to the play. Yang Lingui's review of the conference in the *Shakespeare Newsletter* observed that 'Over the past four or five years [that is, 1989–1993] . . . the number of [Shakespeare] essays has declined' ('Approaches': 56). The anti-Western backlash in PRC government circles in reaction to foreign criticism of the Tiananmen shootings in 1989 clearly had an adverse effect on Shakespeare activity in the years following the clampdown on the democracy movement. Yang does note, however, the positive Western influence on younger scholars in evidence at this

---

[24] Yang Lingui, 'New Chinese Approaches to Shakespeare: An International Shakespeare Conference in Central China', *Shakespeare Newsletter* (Fall 1993): 56.

conference. The younger generation of Chinese Shakespeareans seems more willing than their elders to engage new ideas and chance new approaches.

1994 Shakespeare Festival

A second International Shakespeare Festival, more modest than the first but again with an emphasis on performance, was held in Shanghai in the autumn of 1994.[25] It had originally been scheduled for 1990, but the 1989 events in Tiananmen Square perhaps contributed to its postponement.[26] When it finally did take place, American and Australian theatre companies that had been expected to participate cancelled, citing funding difficulties. PRC, Taiwanese, and other foreign theatre groups, however, were able to stage twelve productions in three languages – English, German, and, to be sure, Chinese. The Festival also sponsored radio versions of *As You Like It* and *A Midsummer Night's Dream*, as well as lectures, seminars, films, and a Shakespeare exhibition.

The host, Shanghai Drama Institute, opened the Festival with a three-hour long integrated version of the two *Henry IV* plays, involving nearly one hundred students and teachers from the Institute. This production highlighted the antics of Falstaff and his gang, but underplayed the historical events and the Hal/Hotspur competition. It emphasized Hal's relationships with his father and Falstaff, and thus had Confucian overtones. The tavern 'underworld' was meant to suggest the decadent West – wigs, as

---

[25] See Li Ruru and David Jiang, 'The 1994 Shanghai International Shakespeare Festival: An Update on the Bard in Cathay', *Asian Theatre Journal* 14 (1997): 93–119; Audrey Stanley, 'The 1994 Shanghai International Shakespeare Festival', *Shakespeare Quarterly* 49 (Spring 1996): 72–80; Yang Lingui, '1994 International Shakespeare Festival', *Shakespeare Newsletter* 4 (Winter 1994): 79.

[26] See Li Ruru's answer to Dennis Kennedy's contention that it was cancelled because of the Tieananmen events ('Bard': 80, n.25).

usual, worn to make Chinese actors look 'foreign'. Falstaff was
played as 'a shabby, turn-of-the-century British colonial'; in the
end, as expected, he is devastated by King Henry's rejection
(Stanley, 'Festival': 77). Li Ruru and David Jiang's review of the
production is confusing. On the one hand, they quote critic Yan
Mingbang approvingly as saying the *Henry IV* contained,

> parallels with what is happening today in our society. Audiences
> can naturally discern a link between their own lives and the
> play . . . The last scene of the production . . . reveals what
> a dirty game politics is, and how ruthless politicians can be.
> Chinese audiences received the message in this scene and wel-
> comed the contemporary relevance.

Yet further along, Li and Jiang write: 'the 1994 Shanghai version
of *Henry IV* was not really interested in conveying any commentary on contemporary society' ('Festival': 100–101).

Another huge Festival undertaking was the staging of the first
Western style opera in China, an adaptation of *Troilus and Cressida*.
The opera was televised in a live broadcast, and impressed most
who saw it. This lavish production featured a full orchestra, two
choirs, and seventeen solo performers. Shakespeare's text was
streamlined to a simplified five-page libretto to allow for arias,
ensemble choruses, and other Western opera features. The production stressed Troilus and Cressida's love story and war's horrible
effect on both individuals and society in general. Audrey Stanley
wrote, 'Certainly the production created a powerful image of the
madness of war and the tragedy of individual lives and aspirations
placed in its path' ('Festival': 75). Yet Stanley also wonders aloud
about the likelihood of a sufficient Chinese audience for Western
style opera. Indeed, the audience even for traditional opera in
China is diminishing, as the younger generation shows little interest
in classical theatre. Thus, it seemed to Stanley a bit misguided
for Chinese adapters to amalgamate two foreign entities –
Shakespeare and Western opera – and expect it to succeed.

Even *yueju* opera, a relatively recent form, cannot attract young
audiences, though currently it is arguably the most popular opera

style of all. The Shanghai troupe that performed *Twelfth Night* at the 1986 Festival offered their version of ·*Hamlet* (retitled *The Prince's Revenge*) in this *yueju* style. Stanley observes that the cuts made to *Hamlet* 'emphasized the love story of Ophelia and Hamlet', and the action was far removed from the politics of Denmark ('Festival': 73). Reduced to nine scenes, this opera plot incorporated Chinese settings, character names, and featured sword dances, a climactic duel scene, and stylized movements in keeping with *yueju* opera conventions. Stanley was much impressed with the set, music, costumes, and skills of the actors, especially Zhao Zhigang who played Hamlet. Li and Jiang also applauded his beautiful singing, and ability to convey Hamlet's emotional conflict concerning his mother ('Festival': 111). On the one hand, Gertrude has raised Hamlet and so should be honoured by him, but, on the other, she has been disloyal to her husband, Hamlet's father, and thus should be condemned. Two stirring arias sung by Zhao apparently brought across this conflict with great force. Both critics and audiences counted *The Prince's Revenge* a huge Festival success. But again the question arises as to how far one can go before Shakespeare is no longer really Shakespeare?

More 'legitimate' Shakespeare was an *Othello* performed as straight drama, employing audience space as well as the stage for its acting area. The action began on Cyprus; that is, with Act II of Shakespeare's tragedy. The setting, probably influenced by Sergei Youtkevich's 1955 film version of *Othello*, was decidedly 'foreign', with Renaissance costumes, architectural set details, and other Italian touches. On the other hand, the actors were not made up to look Western, and Othello was played as a non-Black for the first time on the Chinese stage. Some minor characters were eliminated – for example, Bianca, Lodovico, and Gratiano. Arguably the most singular aspect of this production was Iago positioned as the tragedy's central character, and his point of view offered as a reasonable one. The ensign's frustration with his lot was understandable because he cannot get ahead despite his talents, while Cassio advances in his career because of his good connections. According to director Lei Guohua, Iago's situation was meant to air a common frustration in modern-day China: 'I can see many Iagos in today's society: they are talented and capable, but they cannot achieve the status they deserve. They are therefore jealous; . . . the root of [Iago's] jealousy is the injustice and unfairness to be found in society' (Li and Jiang, 'Festival': 96). To further underline her point, Lei cast a young actor as Iago, and she cut lines and added new ones. As a justification for his actions, Iago has a final speech before he commits suicide (unlike Shakespeare's villain). He begins this soliloquy with self-praise:

Iago, no matter what has happened, you are a resourceful man. You have shaken heaven and earth beyond the battleground, and your wisdom has defeated the reckless courage of a commander. . . . Iago, you have justified your existence. However, Heaven is jealous of your talent, and you are down on your luck. Those who have been chosen by fate are always mediocrities – Cassio, good luck to you! Cassio, I wish you good fortune. (*Iago bursts out laughing and then kills himself.*) (Quoted in Li and Jiang, 'Festival': 97)

This Iago-centred version of *Othello* seemed rather confused to reviewers Jiang and Li. They point out that except for the beginning and end of the tragedy Iago was played mostly straight and villainous, thus making him rather inconsistent taken on the whole.

Another production that went against the grain for a central character was Fudan University's *The Merchant of Venice*. Its aim was to present Shylock as a mostly sympathetic character. Thus, it stressed the conflict between the merchant and the Jew and played down the romantic plot. In one of two alternative endings offered to the audience, Shylock further justifies his usury by presenting to the court his economic viewpoint. In the other, he demonstrates his love and concern for his daughter Jessica, and accepts Lorenzo as his son-in-law. The Fudan production also alluded to the Nazi persecution of the Jews, and added a narrator-guide to help audiences interpret the action. The audience was also invited to suggest alternative 'verdicts' in the court scene, which were then duly rehearsed on stage by the players and presented back to the audience for its approval.

A second *The Merchant of Venice*, performed by the professional Shanghai Children's Art Theatre, was a young person's version. Played mostly for comedy, it stressed the economic issues and eliminated the religious ones. Many of the speeches were simply declaimed to the audience, and the presentation throughout was rather stylized. A hook-nosed, grey-wigged Shylock, recalling a *commedia del'arte Pantalone*, acted a greedy and comic melodramatic villain. Portia, with blond wig and mauve skirt, seemed a stereotypical doll-like heroine. Costumes generally suggested Renaissance Venice, and the piazza and canal set even included an on-stage gondola at one juncture. The play's action ended with the trial scene, but Shylock, in keeping with the production's focus, was not forced to convert. Director Kang Ansheng said that he wished to convey a moral message. He writes in the programme notes: 'We sincerely hope that, as in *The Merchant of Venice*, all the benevolence and beauty in human life will be loved and cherished by people and will further develop, while everything malevolent and ugly will be censured and brought to an end' (quoted in Li and Jiang, 'Festival': 101–102).

Troupes from the UK mounted the Festival's two plays offered in English. *Twelfth Night* was a joint venture of the Salisbury Playhouse and the Royal Lyceum Theatre of Edinburgh. It featured a mostly bare stage with an abstract set. The set consisted of a large, white, revolving box-like structure representing in its turnings and wall adjustments the various play locations. Audrey Stanley found a number of things to admire in the production, but felt the verse 'in general poorly spoken' ('Festival': 79). The Leeds University *Macbeth* was a non-professional, bare bones, experimental piece that included unusual cast doublings. At the beginning of the play, a woman acted the role of Macbeth, a man Lady Macbeth; then, following Duncan's murder, the actors switched roles. The Duncan actor also doubled the Porter, Murderer, and Doctor. This *Macbeth* featured a great deal of stage action, perhaps to the detriment of the play's tragic emotion. Various Chinese touches were added as well; for example, the use of drums and gongs and carefully choreographed movements.

Also performed with a greatly reduced cast of only five actors (three men and two women) was The Youth Theatre of Nuremberg's abridged German-language version of *Romeo and Juliet*, co-titled *Young Love '94*. The bare stage contained only mannequins, draped with the actors' various costumes. Each player acted at least two characters, and again there was some unusual doubling. For example, the actor playing Juliet played Tybalt as well. This production included audience interaction and highlighted the frank sexuality of the play. There was also a significant alteration to Shakespeare's plot: in the end Juliet revives and, with the help of the other characters, causes Romeo to spit out his poison!

Perhaps the most controversial of all Festival productions, however, was the first Taiwanese–PRC joint-venture offering, a play loosely based on *Hamlet* and titled *Shamlet*. Since the play was written by a Taiwanese playwright and was first performed in Taiwan, I will consider it in the chapter about Shakespeare in Hong Kong and Taiwan.

Criticism in the Eighties and Nineties

After the repression of the Cultural Revolution, Chinese Shakespeare criticism flourished again and with renewed energy. However, for the most part the same tired and dogmatic models of Marxist criticism tended to be followed. Cautious academics, many burned by the ten-year terror and earlier attempts to draw out their candid responses and honest analyses, were obviously wary. Hence, they mostly continued to view literature publicly, at least in their published essays, as a weapon in 'class struggle'. Regardless of setting, Shakespeare's plays, according to many Chinese critics, were taken to be about and critiques of early modern England (He, *STCE*: 97). Social themes and heroic model characters were still the analytical focuses. In 1986 He Qixin wrote: 'in most Chinese critical essays only the "political issues" of the play are carefully examined while its other themes are ignored' (*STCE*: 112). He continues elsewhere, thus Chinese critics 'fail to distinguish dramatic art from political treatises and consistently interpret Shakespeare according to a predetermined political formula' ('Trends': 96). Moreover, 'Chinese critics' inadequate understanding of Shakespeare's plays often misleads their readers' (*STCE*: 124). He Qixin summarizes Chinese criticism in the decade or so after the Cultural Revolution as follows:

> Conclusions are usually not drawn from close examination of the text itself but some preconceived concepts of the age of Shakespeare, the playwright's political viewpoints, and his stand on the political issues current in England. But since the hypothesis that Shakespeare was writing for the rising bourgeoisie cannot be verified by reference to historical fact, these discussions of 'political themes' in Shakespeare's plays are not useful in understanding these plays. On the contrary, the political interpretation given by Chinese critics is likely to misdirect attention to ideas of which Shakespeare was doubtless aware but not concerned to dramatize. Accordingly, their criticisms very often miss the essence and dramatic power of the plays (*STCE*: 112–13).

As recently as 1987, on the forty-fifth anniversary of Mao's 'Talks at the Yenan Forum on Literature and Art', Wang Zhen, Vice Chairman of the Chinese Communist Party's Central Advisory Commission, could still say:

> We will firmly implement the Party's principles on literature and art by opposing bourgeois liberalization, achieving new unity through criticism and self-criticism and applying principles of freedom in literary and artistic creation *as long as there is adherence to the socialist road, people's democratic dictatorship, the leadership of the Communist Party, and Marxism–Leninism and Mao Zedong thought* [italics mine].[27]

---

[27] Quoted in Edward Berry, 'Teaching Shakespeare in China', *Shakespeare Quarterly* 30:2 (Summer 1988): 216.

Thus, the signal to Shakespeare scholars continued to be clear.

A significant volume published during the eighties was Fang Ping's *Make Friends With Shakespeare* [*He Shashibiya jiao ge pengyou ba*] (1981), which included seventeen essays written in the late seventies and early eighties. Sui Tianzhang, Sun Jiaxiu, Zhang Siyang, Xu Bing, Zhang Xiaoyang, He Xianglin, and Lu Gusun also contributed major work during the eighties. *Chinese Shakespeare Studies* published a number of journal issues as well, and *Foreign Literature Studies* [*Waiguo wenxue yanjiu*] included significant Shakespeare articles.

Encouraged by translations of classic Western books of scholarship and criticism, China moved slowly from a consideration of exclusively ideological approaches to Shakespeare to relatively 'safe' linguistic studies that went hand in hand with translation. One of my own graduate students, Ju Yumei, wrote her thesis on 'A Stylistic Analysis of *Macbeth*'. Further, while Marxist criticism was still dominant in the eighties, there were a few early attempts to understand Shakespeare's art in aesthetic terms. Along these lines, the playwright's work was often compared with classical Chinese poetry, drama, operas, and novels. However, after the Tiananmen Square episode in 1989, there was a government-inspired campaign to curtail Western influence and promote Chinese culture, and this hostile political climate adversely affected Shakespeare activity for a time (Zhang, *Shakespeare*: 249). The Shakespeare Festival scheduled for 1990 in Shanghai was cancelled, perhaps due to the government's fear that the world media which covered the Tiananmen events would return to expose other PRC problems. But in 1991, with the appearance of Meng Xianqiang's *Shakespeare Criticism in China*, a collection of thirty essays and an extensive bibliography, Shakespeare study seemed once again on track.

Yang Lingui's paper on 'Major Chinese Approaches to Shakespeare in the 1990s', part of a seminar at the 2000 Shakespeare Association of American convention, argues that 'Shakespeare scholars since the late 80s have shown more literary concerns than political interest when they approach Shakespeare'.

Yet Yang goes on to say that 'they still regard Marxism as their dominant theoretical orientation'. This contradiction is reflected in his examples. Yang quotes Zhao Li as studying Shakespeare 'under the guidance of Marxist historical materialism and dialectics' and contends that Sun Jiaxiu's recent work expresses her preference for Marxist approaches. While stylistic and other structuralist approaches have now come into fashion in China, some younger critics, often those who have studied in the West, go even further and employ the latest theoretical approaches. As with scholars the world over, they have become interested in feminist, gender, and post-colonial issues; cultural studies, the new historicism, and semiotics; and can drop appropriate theorists' names and employ their ideas as readily as Western graduate students. Shanghai hosted a 1998 conference organized around the theme of 'Perspectives and Performances of Shakespeare in China', with scholars and theatre people from Taiwan, Hong Kong, Australia, Japan, India, and the US participating. This kind of exposure to the global world of Shakespeare and theatre study will surely broaden the PRC's view of the playwright in the years to come.

Shakespeare in the Schools

Peter Hessler's amusing article in *The New Yorker* about teaching Shakespeare to undergraduates at Fuling Teachers College in Sichuan Province notes: 'Politics is [still] unavoidable at a Chinese college, even if the course is foreign literature, and so my subject became English and American Literature with Chinese Characteristics'. Hessler reports that his students' interpretations of *Hamlet* follow familiar Chinese Marxist critical views: that Shakespeare 'spoke for "the proletariat" [but was a] "petit-bourgeois capitalist" ', that Hamlet 'cared deeply about the peasantry', and so on (13 November 2000: 4).

But what of the history of Shakespeare study in Chinese schools and universities? It began with British and American missionary teaching in the late nineteenth and early twentieth centuries. On and off from the twenties onward to the present day, Shakespeare has been part of the English curriculum of Chinese high schools and universities. As early as 1924, *The Merchant of Venice* was published in English with annotations in Chinese for high school students. Currently Shakespeare is taught in senior middle schools throughout China, though often by way of bio-graphical and historical notes and selected speeches and scenes in Chinese translation. Beginning in 1978, most of the court scene from *The Merchant of Venice* (IV, i) has been included in countrywide high school Language and Literature textbooks.

From 1978 to the present, the PRC's national university curric-ulum, with the official sanction of the State Education Commis-sion [*Guojia jiaowei*], has included Shakespeare courses. The idea is that advanced students of English can enhance their reading abil-ities and general command of the language with literature offer-ings such as Shakespeare.[28] On the university level, both Foreign Language and Chinese departments teach the poet/playwright. At times famous lecturers from abroad have offered Shakespeare courses. For example, poet and critic William Empson (1906–1984) taught Shakespeare in China in 1937, and again from 1947–1953, and Stephen Greenblatt did so more recently. While visiting British, Australian, American, etc. professors give lectures on Shakespeare in Chinese university Foreign Language depart-ments, more and more well-trained Chinese professors teach Shakespeare as well. Some, however, cannot read the Bard in English or do not know English well enough to understand him in the original. As He Qixin points out, this is a big problem, for there is 'considerable distortion in Chinese translations of Shake-speare's plays, bringing misunderstood and [mistaken] interpret-ations to a nation where the majority of the reading public relies heavily upon translations of the plays and critical essays written in

---

[28] See, He Qixin, 'Teaching Shakespeare in Chinese Universities', *Chinese Shakespeare Yearbook, 1994*, ed. Meng Xianqiang, Changchun: Northeast Normal University Press, 1995: 211–24.

Chinese' ('Trends': 96). Add to this that translations do not typically reflect the disjuncture between modern vernacular Mandarin and a Chinese equivalent of early modern English, and the Chinese therefore get a very different sense of Shakespeare than English readers do.

Beginning with the creation of the National Drama Academy in 1935, the various Chinese theatre schools have used Shakespeare as a central part of their curriculum. Shakespeare's plays are required 'texts' at the Shanghai Drama Institute (founded in 1952) and the Beijing's Central Academy of Drama (founded in 1953). A graduation requirement at these institutions is often a public performance of a Shakespeare play. English or Chinese language graduate students may also choose Shakespeare as a thesis or dissertation topic, but even today they must be careful in selecting their subject matter.

The 2000 Verse Translation of Shakespeare's Complete Works

As early as 1989 Fang Ping proposed yet another translation of a complete Shakespeare, but this time with a difference. Unlike the editions of Liang Shiqiu and Zhu Shenghao, Fang would oversee a comprehensive Shakespeare using the 'sound unit' Chinese character groupings to suggest English poetic rhythms, and by doing so honour the poet's verse. As it turned out, Fang himself did most of the translations as well as the introductions, and also monitored the translations he did not do. Although the now octogenarian Fang is one of the most respected Chinese Shakespeareans of his generation, and an energetic translator of many Western texts, he could only interest a small provincial publisher in his project. In 1999 the Hubei Educational Publishing House brought out Fang's twelve volume Shakespeare in a relatively small press run. One year later the Owl Publishing House in Taiwan also published it in a somewhat larger printing. Fang calls his edition the *New Complete Works* (*Xin quanji*) to distinguish it from past versions. It has received generally good reviews so far. Qiu Ke'an describes it as 'an important attempt' at a Shakespeare in verse.[29] But he goes on to say that it is not a good acting edition, and that Fang is not as good a poet as, say, Cao Yu.

---

[29] Qiu's remarks were made to the author in a Beijing interview, 16 June 2002.

CHAPTER FIVE

Shakespeare in Hong Kong and Taiwan

'This island's mine . . .' (*The Tempest* I, ii, 331)

The early history of Shakespeare in Hong Kong is perhaps the earliest history of Shakespeare in China. After the Qing Dynasty's defeat in the so-called 'First Opium War', and following the 1842 Treaty of Nanjing that ceded Hong Kong to Great Britain, the colonizers brought with them to the territory their literary comfort food. That is to say, Shakespeare was imported to Hong Kong to satisfy the British expatriates' hunger for home, not for any notion of cultural exchange. Indeed, in many far-flung English outposts during the latter half of the nineteenth century, the colonizers built theatres to stage their British plays. According to James R. Brandon, both local amateur groups and visiting professional companies played Shakespeare in specially constructed proscenium-arch theatres: ' "Doing Shakespeare" was an unquestioned, if unofficial, thread in the fabric of British expatriate colonial life' ('Shakespeare(s)': 3). In the late nineteenth and early twentieth centuries on the island, the Hong Kong Amateur Theatrical Society, Dramatic Club, and Mummers group staged versions, usually 'burlesques', of a number of Shakespeare plays.[1]

---

[1] See Dorothy Wong, 'Shakespeare in Hong Kong: Transplantation and Transposition', M.Phil. thesis: Hong Kong Baptist University, 1995: Appendix VIII, 167; 46–47.

In order for the island's native population to begin assimilating and to get ahead economically and even socially, it was necessary to learn the colonizer's language. Hence, English education was an important part of the official school curriculum. By 1882 native students attending the Hong Kong government sponsored Central School (later, Victoria College) were reading Shakespeare as part of their study, as a means of teaching them the language and transmitting English values. Some six years later, the playwright/poet appeared as a discrete subject to be tested on school Entrance exams.[2] The Oxford Local Examination, for instance, given to all Hong Kong students for use in determining admissions to British and American schools and later to the University of Hong Kong (established 1912), included questions on Shakespeare (Wong, 'Shakespeare': 29). Shakespeare was thus a factor, along with various other English language and cultural impositions, in strategies for colonizing the islanders. His works represented one important component of British education – that is to say, 'Western elite learning'. Language pedagogy included Shakespeare and other classic British literature, supplementing grammar and written and oral English. Hong Kong Professor Mimi Chan notes a truism, 'Literature is language, and studying language through the study of English literature makes the process more interesting and less dry.'[3] Some Hong Kong instructors even recommended conning Shakespeare's famous

---

[2] Dorothy Wong, ' "Domination by Consent": A Study of Shakespeare in Hong Kong', eds. Theo D'haen and Patricia Krus, *Studies in Comparative Literature* 26: 2 (Amsterdam: Rodopi, 2000): 46, 49. See also Daniel S.P. Yang, 'Shakespeare at Hong Kong Repertory Theater', *Shakespeare in China: Performance and Perspective – A Collection of Theses*, Shanghai: Shanghai Theatre Academy, 1999: 75. Yang indicates that selected scenes and poetry were also featured in high school texts very soon after colonization.

[3] 'Figurative Language in Shakespeare: The Hong Kong Student's Response', *New Studies in Shakespeare*, ed. Ruan Shen, Wuchang: Wuhan University Press, 1994: 252.

speeches and soliloquies as aids to improving colloquial fluency!

Historical circumstances in the first half of the twentieth century, such as the Japanese occupation of the island and the mainland war, had at times a negative effect on English learning and, in turn, on Shakespeare activity. After the Japanese defeat and the Communist victory on the mainland, however, English was perceived as 'the protector's' language and thus took on special importance.[4] During the fifties the Lambs' Shakespeare became common textbook and examination fodder in the schools, and Shakespeare dominated the English Literature syllabus at the then one university in the territory. In the years between 1950 and 1965, The Hong Kong Certificate Examination, an achievement test given to all secondary school seniors, included questions on various plays or the sonnets.[5] At first, the examined play material was taken from the Lambs' plot summaries, but by 1958 students were tested on actual Shakespeare texts. Because of the political climate of the sixties that promoted Cantonese as an 'official' colony language, Shakespeare moved from required to an elective exam subject. But today the playwright/poet is to be found on the English Literature examination for university acceptance. According to Dorothy Wong, Shakespeare is 'seriously studied for entrance to highly competitive universities in Hong Kong' ('Domination': 47).

In 1953 the University of Hong Kong hired celebrated British poet Edmund Blunden to Chair its English Department, and one of his main teaching focuses was Shakespeare. Blunden spent eleven years at the university, and during his tenure he organized a

---

[4] Eugene Chen Eoyang, 'From the Imperial to the Empirical: Teaching English in Hong Kong', *Profession 2000*, ed. Phyllis Franklin, New York: The Modern Language Association of America, 2000: 63.

[5] Wong, 'Shakespeare': Appendix I, 155; Wong, 'Domination': 52.

drama group called 'Masquers' that performed Shakespeare in English. Among their productions were *Twelfth Night* (1956–57), *As You Like It* (1958), *Romeo and Juliet* (1961), *A Midsummer Night's Dream* (1962), and *Othello* (1963) (Wong, 'Shakespeare': Appendix VIII, 167–68). Blunden himself acted Adam in *As You Like It*.[6]

By the mid-fifties, the idea of cultural exchange with the natives living in the British colony took firmer hold. On the Bard's 390th anniversary, the Sino-British Club organized the first ever Hong Kong Shakespeare Festival. This pioneering but modest undertaking included a scene from *Romeo and Juliet* acted in Cantonese, a lecture on Shakespeare and the Elizabethan World, and readings of the sonnets (see Wong, 'Shakespeare': 53–56). Newspaper articles promoting the Festival advocated using Shakespeare as a model for Hong Kong's own drama, and urged writers and directors to create plays in the vernacular combining Western and Chinese conventions.

In addition to the several Masquers' stage productions in the fifties, Radio Hong Kong's English-language station aired *The Tempest* (1954) and *Hamlet* (1955). Around this time as well, the Sino-British Club sponsored a Shakespeare seminar. However, the waning years of the decade were difficult politically in Hong Kong. One consequence was that the annual arts festival was cancelled in 1960, and there was ever-increasing censorship of books and plays in the colony. On the other hand, antique Shakespeare, especially in English, was deemed relatively safe. In the early sixties, for example, Argo Records could release their stock of recorded plays, and, as a prelude to the 1964 Hong Kong Festival to mark Shakespeare's 400th anniversary, the British Council organized a month-long Shakespeare exhibit (Wong, 'Shakespeare': 57–59).

This second Festival was somewhat broader in scope than the

---

[6] Barry Webb, *Edmund Blunden: A Biography*, New Haven: Yale University Press, 1990: 296.

one ten years earlier. In addition to a joint-venture (Hong Kong Stage Club and Garrison Players) *Twelfth Night* performed in English, it featured the first ever Hong Kong Shakespeare production entirely in Cantonese. This milestone was *The Merchant of Venice*, retitled *Weinishi di shangren*, and staged by the Drama Society of the Hong Kong Chinese University. Supplementing the performances were screenings of classic Shakespeare movies in the City Hall, and the sale of commemorative items celebrating the Festival.

From the seventies onward, there were increasing appreciations, reviews, and scholarly criticisms of Shakespeare in the colony. However, arguably the most important measure for tracking the history of Shakespeare in Hong Kong is stage productions. In addition to local amateur and professional groups, British theatre companies, often with British Council sponsorship, mounted a number of Shakespeare plays. The Royal Lyceum Theatre, Bristol Old Vic, Birmingham Theatre, the Chichester Festival Company, Young Vic, and The English Shakespeare Company were among them (see Wong, 'Shakespeare': Appendix VIII, 167–71). In 1970 the British Council together with the Hong Kong Urban Council co-sponsored an event they titled 'The Appreciation of Shakespearean Drama'. The programme included scenes from *The Winter's Tale*, *Hamlet*, *Twelfth Night*, and *Othello* performed by the London Shakespeare Theatre.

There was no 1974 Hong Kong Shakespeare Festival, but 1975 saw a Cantonese *The Taming of the Shrew* [*Xunhaoji*] (also revived in 1976), produced by the Youth Art Amateur Group. However, perhaps the most significant event for theatre Shakespeare in Hong Kong came in 1977, when the Urban Council created the Hong Kong Repertory Theatre, the very first professional company on the island. According to its one-time director Daniel S.P. Yang, over the years this group's Shakespeare productions have been the island's most important to date. Hong Kong Rep has staged some dozen plays so far with ever increasing polish. During its inaugural season, the company mounted Ho Manwui's adaptation of *Hamlet*, with the revised title *Huangzi fucho ji* [*Vengeance of the Prince*], Hong

Kong's initial foray into Shakespearean tragedy.[7] It was acted in Ho's Cantonese prose translation, and Shakespeare's plot was adapted so that Chinese audiences might recall an ancient but widely known tale of incest and fratricide. Shakespeare's characters were given Chinese names, and the *mise en scene* was the Five Dynasty period (907–960) but with Tang Dynasty (618–907) costumes. The play's textual cuts were very severe, resulting in less than half of Shakespeare's *Hamlet* surviving. Eliminated were two of Hamlet's familiar soliloquies, Ophelia's songs, and such characters as Fortinbras and the gravediggers. Most of the longer scenes and speeches were abbreviated, even including the famous 'To be or not to be' soliloquy. Scenes were also altered; for example, the mad Ophelia tries to kill her brother, mistakenly thinking Laertes her father's murderer. Though the Hong Kong Rep attempted a polished professional production, performances were unfortunately rather sloppy, as stagehand noises and missed entrances detracted from the show's quality. The production received mixed reviews (see Wong, 'Shakespeare': 63).

Other late-seventies Shakespeare included *A Midsummer Night's Dream* [*Zhongxiaye zhimeng*] by the Hong Kong Polytechnic Society and the second Hong Kong Rep production, a *Macbeth* retitled *Assassination of the King* [*Shijun ji*]. Chow Yungping translated, adapted, and directed the play. Shakespeare's setting was honoured, but his already brief play was abbreviated still further to about half of its original length.

In the year 1980 the First Generation Drama Club staged a *Twelfth Night*. But the most significant production of that year was Glen Walford's *Romeo and Juliet* [*Luo Miou yu Zhu Liye*] for Hong Kong Rep (see Wong, 'Shakespeare': 66). Walford, then Artistic Director of the newly established Chung Ying Theatre Company,

---

[7] Daniel S.P. Yang, 'Shakespeare at Hong Kong Repertory Theater', *Shakespeare in China: Performance and Perspectives – A Collection of Theses*, Shanghai: Shanghai Theatre Academy, 1999: 76. (Abbreviated as 'HKR' hereafter.)

was the first foreign director to mount a Shakespeare in Cantonese, and, according to Daniel Yang, this production represented the first really professional work done by the Rep ('HKR': 77–78).[8] The textual cuts this time were more modest, but omitted were Mercutio's Queen Mab speech, the sonnet when Romeo and Juliet first meet, and other familiar lines and dialogue.

Hong Kong Rep turned to comedy in 1982 and 1984, staging *The Taming of the Shrew* [*Xunhao ji*] and *The Merchant of Venice*. Yang himself directed both plays and translated Cantonese and Mandarin versions of them in rhyme, with the latter the more successful. As is common in many Western *Shrew* productions, the translator/director cut the Christopher Sly 'induction' scenes and replaced them with a new frame – a company of actors presenting *Shrew* 'as told by Shakespeare some 400 years ago' (Yang, 'HKR': 78). This change, somewhat akin to the musical *Kiss Me Kate*'s narrative, in this case was meant to help distance the audience from the heavy male-chauvinistic action. Yang had Kate played as a 'problem child' seeking freedom, but trapped in a repressive household by an irresponsible father. Petruchio, although some-what rough around the edges, was acted as a skilful psychologist who knew how to tame a difficult woman. Yang's script revision eliminated some 300 lines, in order for the running time to last approximately two-and-a-half hours, comfortable for modern audiences.

The Urban Council organized the 1984 Hong Kong Shakespeare Festival, a mostly fresh air affair celebrated, in part, to inaugurate the new Ko Shan indoor–outdoor theatre. In add-ition to a London-based company's *Twelfth Night*, it featured a Yang-directed *The Merchant of Venice* [*Weinishi di shangren*]. For his original translation, Yang kept Shakespeare's prose as prose and rhymed his blank verse. Employing American designers, Yang claimed that 'Hong Kong audiences saw for the first time a

---

[8] A part-time professional company, the Seals Theatre Foundation, offered a Cantonese *King Lear* [*Li'er huang*] in 1983, directed by Viki Ooi (Wong, 'Shakespeare': 67).

carefully mounted Shakespearean production whose acting, directing, scenery, costumes, accessories, and lighting were of the same standard as those seen at a major theatre company of the Western world' ('HKR': 80). The Festival also included performances of Elizabethan dances, music, and scenes from various Shakespeare plays. Eight amateur and professional drama groups participated (see Wong, 'Shakespeare': 67–68).

The Hong Kong Academy of Performing Arts mounted an interesting *As You Like It* [*Chunfeng chiudu yumenguan*] in the eighties. The settings were an ancient Chinese court, suggested by appropriately painted panels, and the grasslands beyond the Great Wall, suggested by a flock of cardboard sheep (see Wong, 'Shakespeare': 85–87). Minor characters were caricatured to contrast with Rosalind and Orlando, and Robin Hood references were changed to the outlaws from the famous Chinese outlaw novel *The Water Margin*. Rosalind's 'Epilogue' was cut in order for the play's proper happy ending to conform to classical Chinese conventions.

Hong Kong Rep sponsored a 1986 revival of the PRC Ying Ruocheng and Toby Robertson's *Measure for Measure* [*Qingjun ruweng*] that played in two theatres. The costumes, sets, and atmosphere were meant to recall the Vienna of Shakespeare's original play. This production was followed by an *Othello*, directed by Joanna Chan, newly named head of Hong Kong Rep. Chan translated and adapted Shakespeare's tragedy for her Cantonese actors and audiences, setting the play during China's Spring and Autumn Period (770–476 BCE) when the Middle Kingdom was variously divided. Othello was not played as racially 'other', though he was clearly an outsider. Costumed in a period general's garb, this Othello courted the very aristocratic 'Lady Desdemona'. Chan mostly honoured the Shakespeare text, and titled her drama *Jealousy* [*Ji*], changing the character names to reflect the Chinese setting. Unfortunately, the critics found much to fault in this production. John Dent-Young, in the *Hong Kong Standard*, wrote that this *Othello* was 'overloaded with court etiquette in the clichéd style of Chinese TV historical drama, which is enough to bury one of

Shakespeare's most individual characters' (quoted in Wong, 'Shakespeare': 69).

The critics similarly were not kind to a Tsai Chin directed 1988 *Twelfth Night* [*Di Shier Ye*] at the Rep, the text acted in Zhu Shenghao's translation and the play set in a thirties' Hong Kong. Orsino's world was a classical Chinese one, his 'food of love' traditional music, his dress antique; Olivia and Viola's world, on the other hand, were Western, as indicated by their costumes and behaviours. Characters with English names peopled Olivia's household. Thus, while Shakespeare's comedy might suggest a somewhat rigid class society with little social exchange and mobility (though Sir Toby does ~~promise to~~ marry Maria) and confluence, this production posited a happy coming together of the traditional China and the modern West.

In the nineties, with Daniel Yang again at the helm, critics again praised the Rep's efforts. The productions included *Much Ado About Nothing* (1990), *King Lear* (1993), and *A Midsummer Night's Dream* (1997) – all in new translations by Yang (see 'HKR': 82–84). Contributing to the success of these productions was the recently opened and ultra-modern Grand Theatre, a part of the Hong Kong Cultural Centre. Americans with Broadway credits designed *Much Ado*. The play featured a Victorian setting, and was abbreviated by about five hundred lines. Almost twice as many lines were cut from the Rep's *King Lear*, which was set in an ancient England with a Stonehenge motif. This production had two casts, one Cantonese-speaking and the other Mandarin-speaking. The play was performed alternately, the Mandarin version starring Wuhan actor Hu Qingshu who won high praise from the critics. The Cantonese version, on the other hand, received mixed reviews. Yang's *A Midsummer Night's Dream* was very well received, and it was revived in a fresh production for the 2000 Third Chinese Drama Festival in Taipei. In both venues *Dream* played to sold-out audiences of an estimated 30,000 theatregoers. Yang's translation stuck closely to Shakespeare's text and the distinctions between the playwright's verse and prose. But Yang also made some changes: the mechanicals became Hong Kong workers with

Figure 8. King Lear 1993 (Hong Kong Repertory Theatre).

appropriate Chinese tag names; Peaseblossom, Cobweb, and Mustardseed were renamed Spring Orchid, Autumn Chrysanthemum, Summer Waterlily, and Winter Plum-blossom with rewritten lines about these flowers. The translator/director wrote to Professor Jay Halio about his *Dream*: 'it is certainly the largest scale and most sophisticated production of Shakespeare [to date] in the Chinese language'.[9] Yang describes the production as follows:

> [It] was set in a mythical locale with a touch of contemporary Hong Kong. Athens was changed into 'the Capitol', characters in the court wore military uniforms and formal dresses with 19th century flavor, the lovers and the mechanicals wore outfits which could be readily purchased from local stores. The fairies following Titania were four-season flowers, those following Oberon were beetles and insects. Titania's costume resembled a white lily. Oberon was a king beetle, and Puck was a junior version of his image. The setting consisted of a 45-foot revolve with a yin-yang motive if seen from the top.

In addition to Hong Kong Rep, the Chung Ying Theatre Company is the other important professional Hong Kong troupe now doing Shakespeare. Established in 1979 under the auspices of the British Council, but independent since 1982, it has mounted several significant productions to date. For the 1986 Hong Kong Arts Festival it put on a *Twelfth Night* [*Yuanxiao*] set in Tang Dynasty (618–906) Guangzhou. Bernard Goss adapted the play and Rupert Chan did the versified Cantonese translation. Brechtian distancing was a feature of the production. Dorothy Wong suggests that 'It was the aim of Goss' "hyper-realism" to make his audiences realize that the tradition of foreign culture was as strange as the Chinese culture of the past' ('Shakespeare': 93). The critical success of this production might have had something to do with the reviewers' comparative displeasure with Tsai Chin's *Twelfth Night* mounted shortly before (Yang, 'HKR': 82).

---

[9] 'Materials on *Dream* for Jay Halio', unpublished paper.

Figure 9. A Midsummer Night's Dream 2000 (Mandarin version, Hong Kong Repertory Theatre).

Subsequently in 1988, for the Arts Festival, Chung Ying offered *A Midsummer Night's Nightmare* [*Yan*], again adapted by Goss in a Chan translation. This was followed in 1990 by another Festival production, a Chris Johnson directed *The Two Gentlemen of Verona* [*Junzi Haoqiu*]. The play had a late Qing setting during the era of the infamous Madame Xu Xi and various warlords. The verse of the aristocrats and prose for the commoners suggested a class oriented society. On-stage wheelchairs and bicycles marked the division between the old and young. A live dog played Crab.

Hong Kong stage Shakespeare seems poised to reflect the same professionalism and expertise as British or American Shakespeare in the new millennium. One imagines future productions in Cantonese, Mandarin, and English designed for various audiences, and adaptive interpretations that use Shakespeare to comment on local and global issues. It will be interesting to observe what effect Hong Kong's reversion to the People's Republic will have on its Shakespeare.

Shakespeare in Taiwan

The island of Taiwan, like the island of Hong Kong, has a colonial heritage. Occupied by Japan from 1895 through 1945, from 1949 onward it has been the adopted home of the Kuomintang Nationalists who fled to Taiwan after the communist victory on the mainland. At first the native islanders, descendents centuries past of immigrants from China's coastal provinces, were cruelly treated and severely repressed by Chiang Kai-shek's military, and even today they and their families resent the interloping mainlanders. These outsiders were Mandarin-speaking, not speakers of the native Fujian dialect. Like typical colonial imperialists, the Nationalists considered their culture superior to that of the islanders; indeed, they fancied themselves guardians of the 'true' Han Chinese culture. Thus, Chiang's followers brought with them to the island many of the choicest art treasures in order to keep them out of the hands of the communists of the 'New'

China. Further, the local Taiwanese opera was placed in the shadow of Peking opera, regularly mounted by Kuomintang military troupes in the early days of their takeover. Taiwan is not a unified place culturally; it is an island with distinct groups and peoples.

Shakespeare in Taiwan, perhaps partly because of the West's interest in the island, seems more global in orientation than Shakespeare on the mainland. Professor Ching-Hsi Perng, Chair of the National University's English Department and a Shakespeare scholar, sees no really distinctive Taiwanese Shakespeare, with the possible exception of several theatrical adaptations and a few attempts to read Shakespeare from a Chinese point of view.[10] Shakespeare criticism in Taiwan, suggests Perng, includes all current approaches. As for translations, Liang Shiqiu's and Zhu Shenghao's *Complete Works* are both published and available in Taiwan, as is Fang Ping's *New Complete Shakespeare*. *King Lear*, *The Taming of the Shrew*, *Macbeth*, *The Tempest*, and *Hamlet* are among the newest Taiwanese renderings of individual plays. In addition to the important Shakespeare translator and scholar Liang Shiqiu, Chu Limin, Terng Yilu, and Yen Yuanshu can be counted among the prominent older generation of Taiwanese Shakespeareans. Well-known scholars today include Hu Yaoherng, Hwang Meishu, and Professor Ching-Hsi Perng. Perng's essays and conference presentations are significant contributions to the world of global Shakespeare study. Since the eighties, for example, Perng has written about the Sonnets, *A Midsummer Night's Dream*, and presented papers on *The Merchant of Venice* and Chinese *Hamlets*.

To take the modern pulse of Shakespeare in Taiwan, as in the case of Hong Kong, one needs mostly to look at contemporary theatrical productions. Three of these, all adaptations, are of particular interest: *Kingdom of Desire* [*Yuwang chengguo*], a version of *Macbeth* (1986, revived at various times in the nineties and into the new millenium), *Shamlet*, based on *Hamlet* (1994), and *Kiss me Nana*

---

[10] Response to a questionnaire from the author, March 2001.

[*Wen Wo Ba Nana*], an adaptation of *The Taming of the Shrew* (1997, revival in 1999). Each requires comment.

* * *

Kingdom of Desire was the initial offering of the Contemporary Legend Theatre [*Dangdai Chuanqi Juchang*], a troupe established in the mid-eighties to reinvigorate a dying Taiwanese Peking opera tradition.[11] The company's aim was to produce new works based upon Western classics. Interestingly enough, though, as Catherine Diamond points out, *Kingdom of Desire* is not so much an adaptation of Shakespeare's *Macbeth* as it is of Japanese film director Akira Kurosawa's *Throne of Blood* [*Kumonosu-jo*, literally 'Cobweb Castle'].[12] That is, the company adapted an Asian film that had already streamlined Shakespeare's play, and added Chinese flavour and detail. Both the Japanese film and Chinese opera take place in feudal warlord periods. *Kingdom* was set in Qi during the Eastern Chou Dynasty of the Warring States Period (third century BCE). The accompanying orchestra incorporated Chinese drums and other traditional instruments, as well as the singing styles and on-stage acrobatics typical of Chinese opera. Diamond observes, 'Both the play and the film begin with a Buddhist frame', the *Kingdom* prologue stressing 'the futility of all human endeavor' ('*Kingdom*': 119). As in *Throne of Blood*, the Taiwanese opera has only one witch character, a Mountain Spirit crone with long white hair and costumed with flowing sleeves. Like Washizu, the 'Macbeth' of *Throne of Blood*, Aoshu Zheng is marked a warrior by four flags prominently protruding from the back of his costume. When the warlord's murder is discovered at the end of the opera, the flags are surrendered one by one. Aoshu's wife, like Lady Washizu and Lady Macbeth, is the drama's clear villain, who prompts her husband to commit murder. Like Kurosawa's Lady Washizu, Lady

---

[11] Their second offering in 1990 was an adaptation of *Hamlet* titled *War and Eternity*.

[12] '*Kingdom of Desire*: The Three Faces of *Macbeth*', *Asian Theatre Journal* 11:1 (1994): 119.

Figure 10. Macbeth, *The Kingdom of Desire* 1990; revival of 1986 production (Contemporary Legend Theatre, Taiwan).

Aoshu is pregnant, and it is she who argues the necessity of killing Meng Ting, the Banquo character, and his son to contradict the prophesy that Meng's descendents will rule in the future. In her hand-washing scene, Lady Aoshu sings an aria that reveals she has miscarried, and thus is driven to deep despair and madness. There is no 'Macduff' character in the opera to avenge the murder of his family. Aoshu Zheng's own soldiers kill him at the end. As Diamond concludes:

> That the creators of *Kingdom of Desire* did not turn to Shakespeare's text as their primary source but instead applied Beijing opera's techniques to the Japanese adaptation suggests that Asian dramatists are creating a canon of their own in which the relationship with Western sources and approaches is becoming increasingly attenuated ('*Kingdom*': 130).

* * *

Just as a twice-removed *Macbeth* was the impetus for the *Kingdom of Desire* opera, the joint-venture Taiwanese/PRC *Shamlet* again used Shakespeare merely as a launching point for something else. The expropriation of *Hamlet* incorporated an amalgam of mixed cultural references, with reviewers noting that not all of them were perfectly fused. Shakespeare was seasoned with recognizable Taiwanese and mainland prompts. Shakespeare's famous tragedy provided a ground for discussing history, identity problems, the search for meaning in modern life, the social order, and other issues in the several contemporary Chinas. The absurdist worldview presented in *Shamlet* was meant to suggest the Chinese situation in the modern world.

The title '*Shamlet*' recalls *Shamela* [*An Apology for the Life of Mrs Shamela Andrews*], Henry Fielding's 1741 satire on Samuel Richardson's novel *Pamela*. The Chinese *Shamlet* is a black comedy about a failing theatre company, where actors with real life personal problems try to stage a *Hamlet*. They hope that a successful production will solve the company's financial problems and straighten out their lives. Seven scenes of Shakespeare's tragedy are represented in what is the interior play, but these scenes are all

Figure 11. Lady Macbeth, *The Kingdom of Desire* 1990; revival of 1986 production (Contemporary Legend Theatre, Taiwan).

disordered and mixed up. Hamlet's final duel scene is repeated three times. A single actor plays various contradictory roles; the 'hero' Everyman is also the character 'Riffraff' in the play. The frame play is about the actors' lives and problems. One character/ person, for instance, has been exploited by his older brother and now has a bad credit rating, another fears she is being poisoned, yet another has been accused of rape, and still another worries that his wife is in love with another man. Set against these personal concerns is the actors' attempt to stage a *Hamlet* that will save their theatre company. To be sure, everything goes wrong. During the performance actors forget lines and even their assigned roles, since they have played so many characters. The ghost scene becomes farcical. In short, the play's intention is to make a commentary on the absurdity of modern life with its lack of meaningful order and confused identities. This self-reflexive theme suggests both the complexity and emptiness of contemporary society where 'all the world [seems] a stage'. Like Pirandello's 'six characters', the message is that we are looking for someone to make things right, to make sense of meaningless chaos. Even the programme notes to *Shamela* reflected this idea: character names did not always conform to the characters on the stage, and written out plot details deviated from what was actually performed.

*   *   *

With its Shakespeare within a modern, 'real world' framework, *Shamlet* clearly owed a debt to Cole Porter and Bella and Samuel Spewack's *Kiss Me Kate*. So too, and even more so, did The Godot Theatre's *Kiss Me Nana*. The Godot company had mounted *The New Taming of the Shrew* in 1994, a Western-style musical comedy with an original score by a Japanese composer. Also influenced by *Kiss Me Kate*, it focused on Taiwanese male/female relationships and featured local humour and comedy. But *Kiss Me Nana* was a very different venture. Although *Kiss Me Nana's* title is obviously taken from the American musical, *Kiss Me Nana* is less a Broadway musical than a rock opera (that is, more like the 1970 adaptation of *Twelfth Night* titled *Your Own Thing*). It follows the outline of

Shakespeare's plot closely. Aimed specifically at a young audience, much in the manner of many modern Shakespeare films, the cast included well-known Taiwanese popular stars. *Kiss Me Nana* featured strobe lights, actors with fluorescent-coloured hair, *Mission Impossible* (the television show) theme music, 'heavy metal' rock, and more than thirty songs. There was even a rock version of the Taiwanese national anthem to open the show, and the band was on-stage and prominent. The action was meant to reflect current Taiwanese society, and, at the same time, with its choice of Shakespeare's *Taming* as the source play, acknowledge an ever-intruding global popular culture. The stage was set with a bird-cage-like prop to suggest the cultural and family constraints imposed upon Hao Lina (nicknamed 'Nana', Shakespeare's Kate). A projected image of red lips and flowers implied, in the words of Nanette Jaynes, 'what it can be like to be a female in Taiwanese society'.[13] The Petruchio character, Pan Dalong, suggested a modern young man whose macho personae, just as Petruchio's, will be somewhat softened by the play's end. As in Shakespeare's play, Nana and her sister Lisi (Bianca) are contrasting characters. Lisi is a spoiled daddy's girl – fashionable, conventionally beautiful, falsely modest, a materialist who schemes for a rich husband – to contrast with Nana. The older sister is rebellious, a bit masculine, difficult, wilful, but a perceptive feminist. Though almost beyond the usual marriageable age, Nana refuses to play flirtatious games to attract a male suitor. But, of course, Nana turns out to be the very independent and interesting woman that the Petruchio character wants as a mate. With the exception of an added scene that separates the couple in a forest then reunites them romantically, the first act follows Shakespeare's plot closely, but the second act focuses on an attack on wifely submission and macho masculinity. The theme of mutuality in a relationship, to be sure, goes against Chinese tradition, and thus

---

[13] 'Taming the Taiwanese Shrew: *Kiss Me Nana* at the Godot Theatre', *Shakespeare Yearbook 10*, ed. Holger Klein, Lewiston, NY: Edwin Mellen Press, 1999: 491.

was designed to get the attention of the audience. Jaynes concludes that *Kiss Me Nana* presented to its young target audience, 'a mirror containing caricatures of themselves or of the roles that Confucian patriarchal society has created for them' ('Shrew': 502).

* * *

In sum, these three very different contemporary Taiwanese productions suggest a post-modern flexibility when approaching Shakespeare. His work, as we have seen, is not sacrosanct in Taiwan — the Taiwanese do not limit themselves to revering and preserving Shakespeare's originals. The Taiwanese today put the Bard to their own social and cultural uses. And there is a sense of global modernity in their recent approaches.

CHAPTER SIX

Shakespeare and Confucius

'. . . To suck the sweets of sweet philosophy.' (*The Taming of the Shrew* I, i, 28)

Inscribed on a marble slab over Confucius' tomb in Qufu, Shandong Province, is a statement that translates 'Prince of Literary Enlightenment'. While one might expect China's ancient culture to have had a profound effect on Chinese interpretation of Shakespeare, and some few have argued that it has, there is in fact precious little traditional philosophy informing Chinese Shakespeare commentary to the present. The reason may be in part that Chinese Shakespeare is a twentieth-century phenomenon, and the Middle Kingdom's last hundred years has been marked by the almost continual chaos of war, politics, and ideological turmoil. John C.H. Wu's 1936 essay 'Shakespeare as a Taoist' stands out as a pioneering foray into interpreting Shakespeare by way of antique Chinese philosophy.[1] And yet the Taoist notion of *tiandao*, 'the way of nature', and its relationship to *rendao*, 'the way of people', can be seen as similar to, though of

---

[1] See also Chu Pingyi, 'Taoistic Ideas in the Works of Shakespeare', *Studies in English Literature and Linguistics* 4 (1980): 87–109; Frank Vulpi, 'A Taoist Reading of *King Lear*', *Chinese Culture* 33:2 (September 1992): 45–51.

course not precisely the same as, Western Medieval and Renaissance ideas about a perfectly balanced world, harmonious but hierarchical, there to serve man as an ordered model.

The Tang Dynasty (618–907) Confucian, Han Yu (768–824), suggested that *wen yi zai dao*, 'literature conveys the *dao*', an idea affirmed by the Taoist Zhou Dunyi (1017–75).[2] Confucianism places man in a social context with concern and sympathy (*jen*) for his fellow creatures. Yang Zhouhan sees the PRC's pervasive Marxist literary criticism springing from the fertile seedbed of 'Confucianism with its political-didactic orientation, its emphasis on life, its realistic utilitarianism' ('Mirror': 105). Zhang Xiaoyang, too, believes that 'Confucianism is still a large presence in the social and cultural practices of China today, even though it has lost its dominant position of past centuries. It has undoubtedly greatly affected the interpretation of Shakespeare by the Chinese' (*Shakespeare*: 211). Indeed, studies analyzing Shakespeare by way of Confucianism are starting to appear, though Zhang Xiaoyang also sees Confucian echoes in past translations and recent stage interpretations of the plays.

To be sure, Confucianism has had its ups and downs in the turmoil of twentieth-century China. The twilight of the Qing Dynasty brought with it conflicting views regarding the received tradition. In the late Qing, for example, progressive intellectuals felt that promoting old cultural values might unite and strengthen China and reinforce patriotism. However, military and diplomatic humiliations, culminating in Japan's Twenty-one Demands in 1915, demoralized the Chinese and took its toll on the inherited tradition that in part was blamed for the nation's weaknesses. As well, in the twentieth century's early years, students returning from study abroad brought with them new ideas, especially about good government and modern science. The May Fourth Movement, composed of these students and other intellectuals, attacked

---

[2] See, Yang Zhouhan, 'The Mirror and the Jigsaw: A Major Difference between Current Chinese and Western Critical Attitudes', *Representations* 1:4 (1983): 101–107; Wang, 'Politics': 83.

Confucianism as old fashioned and backward looking. Their aim was to dethrone the revered teacher, and get people to see him as just another ancient philosopher and not the preeminent sage. After all, they argued, Confucius' views were regressive. The master promoted *zhong, xiao, jie, yi* (loyalty, filial piety, integrity, morality) and *sangang wuchang* (the three 'cardinal chords'). The latter included the bond between emperor and subject, father and son, husband and wife. There were also the five constant virtues – human sympathy, righteousness, propriety, wisdom, and good faith.[3] While such Confucian values might promote disciplined personal and social conduct, they in turn led to a rigid and autocratic society. Emperors, exercising absolute power, behaved like gods towards the people; women were subjugated without recourse to fundamental rights we now take for granted. The downside of the social harmony prompted by Confucianism was that it compromised individual freedoms for the vast general population.

In the twenties, though, various defenders of Confucianism came forward. After World War I the previously ascendant West lost much of its moral high ground and authority, and the Chinese increasingly viewed modern science and Western capitalism as limited solutions to their own unique and complicated problems. Indeed, at this time the pacifism of Eastern thought now attracted such influential Western thinkers as Bertrand Russell.[4] Furthermore, the thirties added political overtones to Confucianism, as Chiang Kai-shek's New Life Movement espoused Confucian philosophy and its values as a counter to the ever-increasing Communist threat (Louie, *Critiques*: 14–15). In its attempt to reinvigorate a demoralized Chinese nation, this New Life Movement incorporated elements from fascism, Christianity, and Confucianism into a strange ideological hybrid.

---

[3] See, Fung Yulan, *A Short History of Chinese Philosophy*, New York: Macmillan, 1960: 197.

[4] Kam Louie, *Critiques of Confucius in Contemporary China*, Hong Kong: The Chinese University Press, 1980: 13, n. 41.

The Communists were iconoclastic when it came to the tradition, and launched many anti-Confucian campaigns after their 1949 victory on the mainland. In 1954, for instance, they celebrated the 200th anniversary of the death of Hong Sheng, the famous Manchu *anti*-Confucian dramatist (Snow, *Stage*: 6). The Maoist vision of structuring a new Chinese society on the basis of Marxist-Leninist ideals involved dismantling the 'Confucian shop' and anything else that bound the nation to its feudalistic past. The Cultural Revolution, as another instance, brought with it not only general anti-Western feelings but virulent, specifically anti-Confucian attacks. The sayings in Mao's Little Red Book, *Quotations from Chairman Mao*, as compiled by Lin Biao, replaced the popular wisdom of the venerable sage. Ironically, the anti-Confucian campaign of the seventies was the one that connected the master with Lin Biao himself, Mao's heir-apparent general who staged a failed *coup d'etat* and reportedly died in a plane crash while trying to flee China.

Confucianism, however, is so tied to the fabric of Chinese life and culture, so much part of a national and cultural identity, that the various attempts to stamp it out have not been successful. Most Chinese are still patriotic and loyal to the country's leaders and honour the virtues of modesty, humility, and good manners. Children continue to respect parents and elders. Furthermore, Confucianism promotes the tradition that great literature provides a useful tool for conveying moral lessons, and Shakespeare thus serves as a textbook for right behaviour. 'In fact', points out Wang Shuhua, 'Shakespeare and Confucius have often been mentioned together as "sages" ' ('Politics': 76).

* * *

Of the plays that China has especially embraced in its relatively brief encounter with the Bard, two stand out: the tragedy *Hamlet* and the comedy *The Merchant of Venice*. Both have been enormously popular from the very beginning, and are the most translated, produced, and written about of all of Shakespeare's works.

Western style tragedy, in Aristotle's definition or by any other, was unknown in China until the twentieth century. Classical Chinese drama mandates *datuanyuan*, or 'big and happy reunion', for a *surviving* hero at the play's end. Confucian justice demands good to prevail over evil, and reward must be evidenced on this earth and not merely promised in a hereafter. Thus, the ending of *Hamlet* does not conform to the classical Chinese tradition. On the other hand, the importance of familial ties and virtuous personal conduct are the features of *Hamlet* that are congruent with Confucian values. According to the sage, family relationships are the basis of morality – the ones between father and son (*xiao*) and older and younger brother (*di*) being the most significant. These relationships are, of course, central in *Hamlet*. Moreover, as Confucius' disciple implores, 'Conduct the funeral of your parents with meticulous care' (*Analects*: I, 9), and Hamlet is first revealed as very upset by the proximity of his father's funeral and his mother's marriage. Later, after the ghost tells him of Claudius' perfidy, Hamlet struggles to follow the former king's call for revenge, since a man's character, according to *The Analects*, is measured by 'Being good as a son and obedient' (I, 2). The murderer Claudius has violated a sacred trust with his regicide, upsetting the moral order of the kingdom. Consequently he is unable to pray, reminding us of Confucius' dictate: 'When you have offended against Heaven, there is nowhere you can turn to in your prayers' (*Analects*: III, 13). Claudius has also compromised *zong fa*, just succession, since the king's rule should pass to his son and not his brother.

Courage is a major Confucian virtue, and it must always be in the service of morality. A man of wisdom, says the sage, should never be of two minds about right and wrong. Hamlet is clear as to what he must do, but there is supposedly his famous delay. According to Confucius, one must be quick to act. If one fails to carry out a resolution, he therefore fails to keep his word (*xin*). Further, a man should be ashamed to have his words outstrip his deeds; he should put 'words into action' (*Analects*: II, 13).

Hamlet's intellectuality and philosophical bent recall another Confucian dictate: 'never enlighten anyone who has not been driven to distraction by trying to understand a difficulty' (*Analects*:

VII, 8). The prince's struggle to understand himself and his duty – even to madness – and the connection between the external world and his essential self yield a kind of Confucian enlightenment by the end of the drama. When Hamlet agrees to 'play' at swords with Laertes, as arranged by and for his mortal enemy Claudius, the audience or reader may be puzzled for the moment by the prince's willingness to do so. However, according to the sage, the enlightened person 'is not invariably for or against anything' (*Analects*: IV, 10). This suggests the workings of Fate that Hamlet expresses in the following memorable lines: 'There is special providence in the fall of a sparrow. If it [death] be now, 'tis not to come; if it be not to come, it will be now; if it be not now, yet it will come' (V, ii, 219–22). Shakespeare's 'the readiness is all' (V, ii, 222) and Confucius' 'He has not lived in vain who dies the day he is told about the Way' (*Analects*: IV, 8) are closely allied in sentiment.

There is no doubt that *Hamlet* can be seen as reverberating with Confucian echoes. However, to term Hamlet himself as 'a Confucian exemplar' or 'Confucian hero', as Zhang does, is a misleading exaggeration (*Shakespeare*: 213). The prince, for example, is not 'morally perfect', as Zhang contends. Consider his mistreatment of Ophelia, his arranging the murders of Rosencranz and Guildenstern, his disrespectful behaviour toward his mother, his impulsive killing of Polonius. Thus, contrary to Zhang's contention, he does in fact 'drift with the tide of corruption', and is seriously flawed in a Confucian sense (*Shakespeare*: 213–14). One also questions Zhang's reading that Hamlet has 'a strong sense of political responsibility'. The prince seems little concerned with Danish politics and much concerned with revenge and, most of all, himself. And what of the ghost? Confucius is pragmatic and down-to-earth, and refuses even to discuss the supernatural.

The late Professor Lu Gusun, of Shanghai's Fudan University, felt that *Hamlet* was 'conveniently in compliance with the Confucian ethical code demanding filial piety, unquestioning allegiance to the monarch, and constant chastity' ('Hamlet': 54). On the other hand, as Professor Yang Zhouhan points out by way of warning, Confucian and Western ethical ideals are not identical and it may be misleading to treat them as such. The sage's codes are less flexible than, say, feudalistic concepts based on Aristotle or the Great Chain of Being. Yang further argues: 'The Confucian ethical code governing the parent–child relationship is far more stringent than that in the West. Filial obedience is as absolute as parental authority' (*'Lear'*: 258). Thus, one must be careful not to confuse Confucian and familiar Western frames of reference.

Such caution is to be noted for Confucian approaches to *The Merchant of Venice*, one of the most popular Shakespeare comedies in China. *The Merchant* exists in many translations and can trace its theatre history from the very beginnings of Chinese Shakespeare production. The play is taught widely in Chinese high schools (although often focusing only on the courtroom scene at IV, i) and in universities. The reason for the comedy's popularity probably has something to do with its comic–tragic mixed genre, familiar from Chinese drama, and much to do with the stereotypical figures of the cruel usurer and 'clever wench', both part of Chinese folk mythology. But *Merchant*'s popularity also might be because of the play's perceived allegorical dimension rather than its literal meaning. What compelling interest for the Chinese could there be in the playwright's Jews and Christians, either in a traditional Confucian, Taoist, or Buddhist culture or in the atheistic Marxist state on the mainland? I have argued elsewhere that even for Shakespeare's Elizabethan audience the real religious struggle in the comedy may be between allegorized Italian Catholics or sober Puritans and the Anglicans of the established English Church.[5] If Shakespeare's contemporaries might have read Shylock as a devil-Pope or Puritan usurer out to 'do in' the 'true' Protestant Englishman, could not a Chinese reader or audience see in Shylock the 'foreign barbarian', the representative of Western culture, out to exploit the civilized, self-sufficient Chinese as represented by Antonio, Portia, and the other Christians? In any case, Shylock

---

[5] Murray J. Levith, 'Shakespeare's *Merchant* and Marlowe's Other Play', *The Merchant of Venice: New Critical Essays*, eds. John W. Mahon and Ellen Macleod Mahon, New York: Routledge, 2002: 101–4.

and his world is different and a threat in the play. The villain from outside would convert the genteel Christians by means of his bloody 'circumcision' rite, and savage the polite culture. The patient and benevolent Christians would be recognized as Chinese, ever the good hosts even to their enemies. Moreover, Shylock the barbarian is in the end forcefully assimilated into the clearly superior culture.

Zhang, on the other hand, asserts that a primary reason for *The Merchant*'s popularity in China is because it examines the Confucian moral relationship and conflict between *yi*, 'loyalty to one's friends', and *li*, 'personal profit or gain' (*Shakespeare*: 221–22). He argues that Antonio represents the *yi* and Shylock the *li*. This indeed seems an important motif in the drama, but it is not the only play feature that might connect with Chinese audiences or readers sensitive to Confucianism. The master, for example, praised music and even linked it with gentlemanly benevolence: 'What can a man do with music who is not benevolent?' (*Analects*: III, 3). Here we are reminded of the *non*-benevolent Shylock's distain for the music of masques (see *The Merchant of Venice*: II, v, 28–36). The Jew's soberness, too, is clearly slighted in the following lines: 'The man that hath no music in himself,/Nor is not moved with concord of sweet sounds,/Is fit for treasons, stratagems, and spoils;/ . . . Let no such man be trusted' (V, i, 83–88).

Confucius stressed strict observance of the 'rites', the rules of behaviour and order handed down from generation to generation. He does, however, acknowledge that each age may change the code somewhat to reflect changing times: 'The Yin built on the rites of the Hsia. . . . The Chou built on the rites of the Yin' (*Analects*: II, 23). Thus, the Jewish morality of a previous time may be recognized in Shakespeare's play as an outmoded code, one that has been modified for the better by Christian values. Additionally, Confucius advocates a middle way between vindictiveness and generosity, as does Shakespeare in his comedy. Shylock is humiliated by the Christians, loses his daughter and his money, is forced to convert. While mercy is an important motif in *The Merchant of Venice*, the Christians are not totally merciful. Confucius asks, if you 'Repay an injury with a good turn . . . What, then, do you repay a good turn with?' (*Analects*: XIV, 34). However, Shylock's life *is* spared – perhaps so he might be 'saved' – even after he would have killed Antonio in a most cruel manner. Both a familiar Confucian and Christian tenet is to 'do unto others as you would have them do unto you' (see *Analects*: XII, 2).

Just as *Hamlet* and *The Merchant of Venice*, *Romeo and Juliet* and *Othello* are also favourite plays in China. These dramas present socially or culturally inappropriate marriages that lead to tragedy and death. In a society where traditional arranged marriages are only a generation or two away for many and still practised by some, especially in the countryside, Romeo and Juliet's predicament is especially relevant to the Chinese. Similarly, Othello is a foreigner from an exotic land, beloved by the beautiful native woman Desdemona. The PRC's 'open door' policy, encouraging people from many countries to study, work, and/or live in the Middle Kingdom, and Chinese students and citizens to travel abroad, has made real the threat of interracial and intercultural marriages. In the mid-1980s, a widely publicized news story told of African and Chinese students and the police clashing in Beijing, Nanjing, and Hangzhou, mostly because black men were dating Chinese women and not treating them properly. Edward Berry's Chinese students suggest that *Othello* 'provides warnings against inter-cultural marriages'. They add the play also cautions 'against jealousy, against impatience, against trusting evil companions' (Berry, 'Teaching': 215). And it warns about intemperance. Cassio's alcohol intolerance recalls Confucius' statement about the need for a gentleman to be able to hold his drink (*Analects*: IX, 16), and never drink 'to the point of becoming confused' (*Analects*: X, 8). Iago's hypocrisy is captured in Confucius' observation: 'Cunning words, an ingratiating face and utter servility, these things, Tso-ch'iu Ming found shameful. I, too, find them shameful. To be friendly towards someone while concealing one's hostility, this Tso-ch'iu Ming found shameful. I, too, find it shameful' (*Analects*: V, 25).

Macbeth and Lady Macbeth, of course, are similarly

hypocritical. They pretend to be caring hosts when King Duncan visits their castle, but they murder their royal guest. Lady Macbeth echoes the witches when welcoming the king to her castle: 'All our service/In every point twice done, and then done double,/ Were poor and single business to contend/ Against those honors deep and broad wherewith/ Your majesty loads our house' (*Macbeth*: I, vi, 14–18). Macbeth himself reasons the irrationality of the proposed regicide: 'He's here in double trust:/ First, as I am his kinsman and his subject,/ Strong both against the deed; then, as his host,/ Who should against his murtherer shut the door,/ Not bear the knife myself' (I, vii, 12–16). Macbeth turns out to be a most un-Confucian character: he is ruled by his wife, he murders his king, and even kills his good friend Banquo.

Another tragedy, *Julius Caesar*, was a very popular play before the founding of the People's Republic in 1949, existing in five different translations and praised by China's celebrated modern writer Lu Xun. However, its ungenerous depiction of the gullible and fickle masses obviously forwards the wrong message in a communist state, thus its popularity has waned on the mainland. *Coriolanus*, too, as might be expected, has been rarely produced in the PRC, and Chinese comment on the play is scant. The motif of a dominant mother and her obedient son, though, seems very Chinese, and *Coriolanus'* Roman background could be adapted easily to a Chinese warlord period in the manner of the late Akira Kurosawa's films. But again, the elitism of Coriolanus and Volumnia, and the view of the masses as ignorant, selfish, corrupt, and easily manipulated are contrary to Mainland China's political ideology. Like Coriolanus, Confucius is wary of the common people (*min*) and feels that they are limited. He observes: 'The common people can be made to follow a path but not to understand it' (*Analects* VIII, 9). On the other hand, the sage advises, one should be generous [*hui*] to the common people (*Analects*: V, 16). A man 'should love the multitude at large (*chung*) but cultivate the friendship of his fellow men [*jen*]' (*Analects*: I, 6). A distinction is apparent here between the masses and one's fellow elite. Also relevant to Shakespeare's character Coriolanus is Confucius' advice: 'Be sure to go carefully into the case of the man who is disliked by the multitude' (XV, 28).

*   *   *

King Lear, a family tragedy exploring shifting values, among other issues, also recalls *The Analects*. As we have observed, Confucius teaches that what was acceptable in a previous age is not necessarily to be followed in a current circumstance. There is an awareness that the codes and rites must keep pace with evolving ideas. Thus, King Lear's gift of his lands and powers to his daughters before his death may not necessarily be a bad idea according to the sage. However, what is clearly a Confucian mistake in the play is the two evil daughters' unfilial behaviour. Conversely, Cordelia's first action of criticizing her father's plan may be justified in Confucian terms. Confucius recommends, 'In serving your father and mother you ought to dissuade them from doing wrong in the gentlest way. If you see your advice being ignored, you should not become disobedient but remain reverent. You should not complain even if in so doing you wear yourself out' (IV, 18). Cordelia causes her father to lose 'face', because she refuses to respond appropriately in the king's public court to Lear's ritual ceremony of dividing up his kingdom. Kent, too, defies his monarch. However, his loyalty reminds us of how Confucius' good subject should behave: 'Make sure that you are not being dishonest with [your lord] . . . when you stand up to him' (XIV, 22). And we think of the bastard Edmund when we consider the love he owes his father and the respect he owes to his older brother.

But older brothers, in turn, have responsibilities. In *As You Like It*, Orlando complains, justly in Confucian terms, that his brother Oliver neglects his duty to educate him. D.C. Lau writes that Confucius believed, 'It is not enough for a man to be born with good native substance. A long process of nurture is necessary to give him the breeding that is indispensable to the gentleman.'[6]

---

[6] 'Introduction' to *The Analects* of Confucius, Harmondsworth: Penguin Books, 1979: 38.

This is in essence what Orlando complains about to Oliver when he says, 'You have train'd me like a peasant, obscuring and hiding from me all gentleman-like qualities' (*As You Like It*: I, i, 68–70). Further, Confucius argues that 'we should hold the young in awe', since we cannot know what they will achieve in their maturity (*Analects*: IX, 23). The master, we are told, was willing to take on any student, no matter what his social status, so long as he was hungry for knowledge. The emphasis is on an individual's desire for learning. Education is also, of course, one of Shakespeare's important themes. Additionally, Shakespeare's picture of human relationships in his 'green world' outside the court in *As You Like It* corresponds with Confucius' social ideal. Servant and master, duke and subjects, 'cousins', friends, and ultimately brothers behave with proper deference and responsibility.

Confucius, to be sure, had a lot to say about kingship and good government, as did Shakespeare in his history plays. Medieval feudalism and Chinese feudalism, though different, have much in common. Some aspects of the emperor ruling by the 'Decree of Heaven' (*t'ien ming*) and the king by 'Divine Right' seem similar. Both suggest a higher power concerned with human affairs, and that a heavenly ordained ruler should promote the people's general welfare. The Chinese emperor loses his heavenly mandate when his concern for his country gives way to his own selfish interests. He is then to be replaced by someone more worthy. Shakespeare's *Richard II* is in part a play about a king believing in the absolutism of his divine right, but then being forced to confront a world of changing values. John of Gaunt's 'swan song' points out that Richard's actions compromise his divine mandate. He has 'leas'd out' his kingdom to raise money for his extravagances (*Richard II*: II, i, 59). The sage teaches: a ruler should 'Ensure that those who are near are pleased and those who are far away are attracted' (*Analects*: XIII, 16). The Duke of York, Richard's uncle, among other nobles, is perplexed by his nephew's behaviour. When Richard seizes Gaunt's estate, York asks how Richard can be king if he denies Bolingbroke his just inheritance: 'Take Herford's rights away, and take from Time/ His charters, and his customary rights;/ Let not to-morrow then ensue to-day;/ Be not thyself; for how art thou a king/ But by fair sequence and succession?' (*Richard II*: II, i, 195–99). And what of Richard's histrionic and emotional personal behaviour? Confucius teaches, 'If a man is correct in his own person, then there will be obedience without orders being given; but if he is not correct in his own person, there will not be obedience even though orders are given.' (*Analects*: XIII, 6). Although Bolingbroke's motives might be questionable, in *Richard II*, he is characterized as more worthy to be king than Richard himself.

Similarly, Prince Hal satisfies Confucius' ideas on several counts. In two places in *The Analects* the master says, 'Do not concern yourself with matters of government unless they are the responsibility of your office' (VIII, 14; XIV, 26). The young Hal seems irresponsible at first, but reveals his plan to come out from behind the clouds when the occasion demands, 'And pay the debt I never promised' (*Henry IV, Part 1*: I, ii, 209). He has a programme of study to prepare himself for his eventual 'office' and 'official career' (see *Analects*: XV, 32). On the other hand, Confucius would have harsh words for Hal's pal Falstaff: 'To take pleasure in showing off, in a dissolute life and in food and drink is to lose' (*Analects*: XVI, 5). Moreover, 'To send the common people to war untrained is to throw them away' (*Analects*: XIII, 30), a clear indictment of Falstaff's 'press' in the *Henry IV* plays. Falstaff views his recruits as merely 'food for powder, food for powder, they'll fill a pit as well as better' (*Henry IV, Part 1*: IV, ii, 65–67).

Henry V is viewed by the Chinese as Shakespeare's idealized ruler, akin to the greatest Chinese emperors of the past (see Chen, 'Political': 141–58). A monarch's benevolent paternalism, recommended by Confucius, is evident in Henry's character. The king is concerned with both his peers and the common people. In *Henry IV, Part 2*, he endorses the previous actions of the Lord Chief Justice, which included his own disciplining, and as king rejects the dissolute Falstaff. When the Duke of Ai asked Confucius for advice, he responded, 'Raise the straight and set them over the crooked and the common people will look up to you.

Raise the crooked and set them over the straight and the common people will not look up to you' (*Analects*: II, 19). Shakespeare's Henry V, like Tzu-ch'an, was a 'gentleman on four counts': 'he was respectful in the manner he conducted himself; he was reverent in the service of his lord; in caring for the common people, he was generous and, in employing their services, he was just' (*Analects*: V, 16).

Reading Confucius alongside Shakespeare is, to be sure, an academic exercise. However, one is struck with the many correspondences that can be found. Why then have Chinese critics shied away from this approach, which seems so natural for them to pursue? As we have noted, twentieth-century politics has a lot to do with it, but one hopes that in the future this fertile avenue of analysis will be further explored. It might give Shakespeareans the world over valuable new insights.

CHAPTER SEVEN

The Paradox of Shakespeare in the New China

'That ends this strange eventful history . . .' (*As You Like It* II, vii, [164] 64)

As we have observed, Shakespeare in China is a twentieth-century phenomenon clearly buffeted by the strong winds of Chinese political change. One may legitimately wonder why, of all foreign writers, socialist China has so embraced Shakespeare, a dominant Western cultural icon who can be associated with hated colonial imperialism. For old China, unquestionably, Shakespeare is a potent symbol of Britain, the same Britain of the Opium Wars, the Boxer Rebellion, and the Unequal Treaties. Moreover, in the new China the man Shakespeare was indisputably a bourgeoisie capitalist, owning shares in his acting company and purchasing New Place, the second biggest house in Stratford, among other ventures. Indeed, it is curious to some that in one year the return of Hong Kong is wildly celebrated and in the next yet another Shakespeare conference is held in Shanghai.

From the beginning, as we have seen, China has had a schizo-phrenic love/hate relationship with Shakespeare. For much of the century-and-a-half after the first Opium War, the Middle Kingdom has been at times wary of the intrusion of Western culture, seeing it as yet another instrument of 'foreign devil' domination. On the other hand, now in China, according to a recent book-length study in English, Shakespeare 'is considered the god of art. For the reading public, his writing is regarded more highly than that of any other Western author' (Zhang, *Shakespeare*: 13). Or, as Sun Jiaxiu affirms, in China Shakespeare's work is considered 'the great paragon of dramatic art of all ages' ('*King*': 75). Early in his career Lu Xun argued that his country needed a Shakespeare-like writer to give voice to China's national spirit, adding, 'if a country or nation wishes to endure, a writer like Shakespeare . . . is required' (quoted in Meng, *Survey*: 4). However, Mao Zedong, though a poet himself, had very definite views on the political and propagandistic purposes of art, and had it not been for Marx, Engels, and Russia's love for Shakespeare there conceivably might not be any Chinese Shakespeare today. As noted earlier, big plans were made in 1964 to celebrate the 400th anniversary of the poet's birth, including publication of a complete Shakespeare, but these activities were cancelled as they fell on the eve of Chairman and Madame Mao's Cultural Revolution. During this chaotic period many Chinese Shakespeareans suffered, and Shakespeare himself 'was classified in a category to be purged, and his works – labeled "feudalist", "capitalist", and "revisionist" – were criticized and denounced' (Meng, *Survey*: 34). His books were removed from bookstores and libraries and were banned; no productions of his plays or showing of films based upon them were allowed.[1] Nanjing University professor Chen Jia was publicly criticized and 'struggled against' for crimes that included performing scenes from Shakespeare with his students, one of the many persecutions for 'errant behavior' during this troubled time (Meng, *Survey*: 33).

Yet today Shakespeare is taught in Chinese schools and universities. He is the focus of a scholarly journal (the first to be devoted to a foreign writer), the subject of a national society and provincial ones, the stimulator of theatre festivals and scholarly conferences, and the generator of a thriving book publishing and

---

[1] He Qixin, 'China's Shakespeare', *Shakespeare Quarterly* 37: 2 (Summer 1986): 154–155.

translation industry. He is undoubtedly the most recognized and honoured foreign writer in China. Americans were told when Jiang Zemin visited the United States in 1997 that the Chinese president loves Shakespeare and can quote him.[2] On a more recent state visit to England, his hosts took Jiang to sites in Stratford-upon-Avon and Shakespeare's Globe in London, presumably at the president's request. Zhou Enlai, Hu Yaobang, and other important political leaders from the past also seem to have known and enjoyed the Bard (Zhang, *Shakespeare*: 113, 122, 205–206).

In recent times, however, Shakespeare continues to be buffeted by the political currents in the People's Republic of China. Consider, for example, the case of two translators of Shakespeare's complete works, Liang Shiqiu and Zhu Shenghao. The former, attacked by Lu Xun and Mao Zedong himself, was until quite recently reviled, while the latter, who died young was portrayed as something of a culture hero. This hero and villain mentality has had its effect on the reputations of Liang Shiqiu and Zhu Shenghao in the not too distant past. Professor Liang's edition, published in 1967, for many years was not available on the mainland because of the translator's politics, while Zhu's life and work has been sentimentalized into a 'model comrade' story. Like Lei Feng, the soldier who died young in the cause of Mao Zedong and the Party, Zhu Shenghao is held up as an example of selfless devotion to the revolution for his Shakespeare translation! Contemporary Chinese literature, too, is full of peasants and workers labouring for and often sacrificing their lives in the interests of the 'people'. Zhu and his wife would have us believe the Shakespeare translator was just such a martyr. Indeed, one effusive critic writes, 'The unswerving dedication of Zhu Shenghao is truly remarkable, and he is surely an heroic figure', adding that Zhu's translation is 'a tremendous achievement' (Meng, *Survey*: 21, 23). A conference to honour Zhu was held in Shanghai in 1992.[3]

---

[2] *Time*, 27 October 1997: 58; Zhang, *Shakespeare*: 206.

[3] See Yang Lingui, 'Chinese Commemorate Translator of Shakespeare', *Shakespeare Newsletter* 42: 2 (Summer 1992): 22.

To a large extent modern China has not met Shakespeare on his own terms, but rather has used him to forward a national political agenda. We have seen this at work in Mao's vilification of one of his translators and what could be viewed as the heroic sentimentalization of the other. But scholarship too has been affected by the political climate, perhaps even more so than translation. Many middle-aged and older scholars, remembering what happened to intellectuals on the 'wrong' side during the 1957 Anti-rightist Campaign or the Cultural Revolution, continue to strive hard to be 'politically correct'. A few brave ones, on the other hand, study Shakespeare without preconceived ideological notions, as have most scholars the world over. Two recent Chinese Shakespeare scholar-critics, both of whom are affiliated with mainland universities (one now retired from Northeast Normal University and the other the Vice President of Beijing Foreign Studies University), demonstrate this division. Comparing the work of these men is instructive.

Professor Meng Xianqiang's *A Historical Survey of Shakespeare in China*, published in English translation in 1996, and which I helped translate (though published while still in draft), is a good example of a 'safe' and politically correct Chinese Shakespeare study by an older scholar. In reviewing the history of Shakespeare in China, it emphasizes a recurring theme: that China needs to develop a distinctive approach to Shakespeare based upon Marxist readings. It completely ignores, for example, China's rich Confucian tradition to iterate again and again that politics and ideology is the sum and substance of Shakespeare study. And it raises implicitly the more general question of the value of a strict nationalistic approach to a world literary figure.

Meng's history sounds at times like an economic report. The professor notes that Shakespeare scholarship has flourished under China's communist regime: since 1949 'the number of Shakespeare studies is close to 1000, or eight times the total during the pre-liberation years', and 'more that 2,000,000 copies of Shakespeare's works have been printed since the founding of the People's Republic' (*Survey*: 41, 37). Meng informs us that

Shakespeare criticism developed 'In concert with China's policy of expanding economic reform', and the many publications reflect the energy of China's socialist cultural enterprise (*Survey*: 41). As if some sort of economic productivity goal is the issue in Shakespeare publications!

What seems even more naive and simplistic, however, is Meng's call for 'Shakespeare studies with Chinese characteristics', a clear echo of Deng Xiaoping's slogan 'Socialism with Chinese Characteristics'.[4] Meng thus applies political clichés with familiar diction to Shakespeare activity:

> Chinese Shakespeareans must make a more concerted effort to work together to shape a characteristically Chinese perspective on Shakespeare. . . . The history of Shakespeare in China over roughly the past century reflects its special place in the struggles of the Chinese people. Under the current political and economic reforms and the Government's 'open door' policy, Shakespeare studies . . . [aim] at becoming a component in the nation's socialist cultural construction (*Survey*: 44).

From page one of his *Historical Survey*, Meng sounds all the bromides we associate with political propaganda. Western scholars might find puzzling the logic of Meng's statement that China's 'socialist modernization allows us to continue to make positive contributions to international Shakespeare research' (*Survey*: 1). Furthermore, Meng seems most often to be addressing a Chinese and not a wider scholarly audience.

The question of audience is a relevant one. Much of Chinese Shakespeare criticism seems inwardly directed – that is, addressed to other Chinese scholars or maybe even political leaders who share the same prejudices. Broader scholarly conversations are mostly distorted or ignored. Canadian Edward Berry writes of

---

[4] As Yang Lingui notes, ' "Chinese characteristics" mean[s] mainly Marxist studies, seen through Chinese lenses.' ('Major Approaches to Shakespeare in the 90's'; paper presented at the Shakespeare Association of America Conference, 2000.)

teaching Shakespeare students in China: 'Political issues . . . affect directly the academic careers of the students and thus necessarily determine the future development of Shakespearean scholarship and criticism . . . Certain topics, I was assured repeatedly, would have little chance of acceptance [for an M.A. thesis]; others would be accepted only if pursued in a carefully circumscribed manner' ('Teaching': 215). Zhang Xiaoyang affirms that Chinese professors teaching Shakespeare will focus on social and historical issues in a given play and the ideological in Shakespeare (*Shakespeare*: 193). Meng dedicates his *Historical Survey* to the Sixth World Shakespeare Congress, yet his audience is also, and even mostly, clearly local.

Turning now to an earlier study (1986), we can observe a pioneer who, unlike Meng, is courageous in addressing a wider scholarly audience. He Qixin's unpublished Kent State University doctoral dissertation 'Shakespeare Through Chinese Eyes' (condensed and adapted as 'China's Shakespeare' in the *Shakespeare Quarterly*), though now somewhat dated, is the single best work in English that I know of about Shakespeare in China. It is informative, insightful, and covers in a careful and skilful manner the history, 'mainstream Shakespeare criticism', and translations to the moment when it was written. Most of all, it is relentless in hammering home its major thesis: that the Chinese political and ideological approach to Shakespeare is misguided, causing distortions in translations, productions, and criticism. It is a brave study that challenges elders and names names.

Noting that authentic Shakespeare criticism in China did not begin until after the founding of the People's Republic, Professor He observes that the same principles followed for modern Chinese literature have been adopted by most Chinese Shakespeare critics. 'According to these principles, literature is subordinate to politics; any form of literature is aimed at propagandizing for a special class of people in the society, and each author is consciously or unconsciously writing for his own class' (*STCE*: 31). Such dictates arise, as we have observed, from Mao's 'Talks at the Yenan Forum on Art and Literature'. Professor He concludes: 'the rigid limitations of this political and ideological approach to Shakespeare often hinder Chinese critics and result in biased and unsatisfactory interpretations of Shakespeare's plays' (*STCE*: 31–32). Chinese critics, contends He, sometime misunderstand Shakespeare and thus mislead their readers (*STCE*: 124).

It is not necessary to rehearse in detail all of He's examples – a few in passing will do. He attacks, among others, Bian Zhilin who contends that 'Shakespeare was writing for the people, not for the ruling class, and that Shakespeare opposed the feudal system in the early part of his career and exposed the evils of capitalism in the later' (*STCE*: 17).[5] Professor He considers Bian's 1956 *Hamlet* essay as 'distasteful' because it 'goes to the extreme of "creating" [Hamlet as] a heroic figure who resembles the larger-than-life, type of hero in modern Chinese literature . . .' (*STCE*: 119). Further, Bian is close-mindedly dismissive 'of the utterly absurd and reactionary remarks of modern bourgeois critics'; that is to say, Western ones (quoted in He, *STCE*: 29, n.51). Fang Ping, too, who oversaw the new verse translation of a complete Shakespeare, comes under attack for his view that in *Romeo and Juliet* 'We must emphasize the anti-feudal significance of the love . . . this is not the tragedy of individual lovers, but the tragedy of those who are far ahead of their times and who are willing to sacrifice themselves for their ideological belief' (quoted in He, *STCE*: 89). Fang also feels 'the glorification of Antonio in *The Merchant of Venice* reflects the limitation of Shakespeare; after all, Shakespeare was writing for the bourgeoisie' (He, *STCE*: 109).

Fang Ping and Bian Zhilin are both respected translators of Shakespeare, as well as critics, but He Qixin suggests their ideological approach colours and distorts their translations. Indeed, he argues, most Chinese critic-translators have this same problem: 'the translator's task is often complicated by China's political and

---

[5] Zhang argues, incredibly, that Bian's essays are 'Confucian in principle and spirit, although some are discussed under the label of Marxism' (*Shakespeare*: 215). Wang Shuhua's thesis notes a change in Bian's views over time ('Politics': 116).

ideological approach to Shakespeare; an unbalanced interpretation of a play leads to inaccuracy of rendition and infidelity to the original' (*STCE*: 128). Since some Chinese scholars cannot read Shakespeare in English, Meng for instance, and must rely on translations, their views are in turn corrupted by slanted renderings.

For obvious political reasons, Chinese Shakespeareans have celebrated and elevated an inferior play and have neglected or distorted better ones. *Timon of Athens* is almost universally described as Shakespeare's weakest tragedy, and its rough edges and inconsistencies are well documented, suggesting a collaborator or an unfinished effort.[6] Yet Yang Hui's introduction to his Chinese translation of *Timon* calls it 'Shakespeare's most important work', adding that it is critical to an understanding of Shakespeare, his age and society. Zhang affirms his 'country's enthusiasm for *Timon of Athens*' (*Shakespeare*: 223). Not one but two productions of the play were staged at the 1986 Shakespeare Festival in Shanghai. These productions, according to Zhang, 'were deliberately designed to represent conventional moral concepts and a serious social problem in contemporary China – the prevalent worship of money since the beginning of the economic reform' (*Shakespeare*: 116). The reason for *Timon's* popularity in China is easy to discern: Marx and Engels cite this play in their work to demonstrate how money functions in a capitalist society (Zhang, *Shakespeare*: 223). And former President Jiang Zemin quotes from it 'to point out the harm of money worship and the importance of combating it' (Zhang, *Shakespeare*: 206). On the other hand, only two of Shakespeare's tragedies were *not* produced during the 1986 Shakespeare Festival: *Julius Caesar* and *Coriolanus*. Neither were these plays staged during the 1994 Shanghai Festival. The reason is most likely, again, political. Shakespeare clearly depicts the malleable masses in these plays;

---

[6] See, *Timon of Athens*, ed. H. J. Oliver, London: Methuen, 1959: xxii–xxviii.

they are ignorant, changeable, foolish, and easily manipulated. It is absurd to suggest, as Meng does, that this 'view actually derives from Western Shakespeare Criticism' alone (*Survey*: 14).

In the enormously popular 1981 production of *Measure for Measure*, directed by Toby Robertson and staged by the Beijing People's Arts Theatre, more than five-hundred lines, mostly dealing with sex, religion, and politics were cut (He, *STCE*: 23, n.38; 157–58). Indeed, from the very earliest Shakespeare productions on the Chinese stage, radical adaptations have been common. As in the West, it has been usual for lines and speeches to be dropped or added, but often the motivation for PRC textual alteration has been ideological (He, *STCE*: 158–60). Titles of plays and character names, too, have been routinely changed. No one these days would argue with adapting Shakespeare to present (or future or past) worlds or cultures, or experimenting with various stage techniques. However, the Chinese have increasingly appropriated and expropriated Shakespeare, turning his plays into something radically different – for example, Beijing, *kunju*, *huangmei*, and *shaoxing* operas. This, of course, gives rise to the question of whether Shakespeare is a source or inspiration, rather than authentic 'Shakespeare'? Zhang notes, in a *shaoxing* opera production titled *The Revenge of the Prince* (*Hamlet*), 'the director and adaptor ... staged the play ... without worrying about the loss of a Shakespearean style' (*Shakespeare*: 250–51). Furthermore, Zhang adds, 'many broad-minded Chinese Shakespeare critics, directors, and performers advocate presenting Shakespeare's plays in the form of traditional Chinese drama' (*Shakespeare*: 133). Four plays during the 1986 Festival were so staged and several in 1994. Beyond these adaptations, moreover, China has offered, again in the words of Zhang, 'a style of their own and successfully created a Chinese Shakespeare on the stage ... sinicized versions of Shakespeare's plays' (*Shakespeare*: 114, 130). And it has used the Bard to reinvigorate its own traditional theatre: 'Shakespeare has greatly affected traditional Chinese drama and infused new blood into an old dramatic tradition. ... Perhaps Shakespeare's greatest contribution to China lies in the effect he has had on the vitaliza-

- early translation + Mao (9-10)
- problems with "be" (13)
or "nothing"
- funny titles (from Lambs) (15-16)
- first original text +
performance (17)
- esp. interesting Taoist take (21)

2. Shakespeare + Mao
   1949-1866
- Chinese — and Russian Marxists
  (26)
- Mao (29)

3 Cultural Rev

4 1976-2000
  1986 sh. festival
- hilarious subst. for
  "clamplig boy" (76)

5 Westerners teaching in
China: Empson (1937, 1947-53)
weelblott (early 80s?),
Peter Hessler's funny
anecdote (87-90?)

7 Hy Kong + Taiwan

aiwan: adaptation of Kurosawa's
-ilm → Macbeth

BARNARD

Barnard College • Columbia University
3009 Broadway • New York, NY 10027-6598

Memorandum

To:

From:

Subject: Date:

tion of traditional Chinese drama' (Zhang, *Shakespeare*: 13, 251; see also 130–172 *passim*).

After the so-called 1989 Tiananmen 'incident', the People's Republic government launched a campaign to promote traditional Chinese culture and inhibit Western influence. Some say this resulted in the postponement of a Shakespeare Festival planned for 1990 (Li, 'Bard': 80, n.25). But in 1993 an international Shakespeare conference took place in Wuhan, in 1994 a Shakespeare Festival was held in Shanghai, and in 1998 still another in Shanghai. Fang Ping published his verse translation of the *New Complete Shakespeare* in 2000. As Zhang observes, recently Shakespeare seems everywhere in the New China: 'Shakespeare has permeated Chinese life like no other great Western cultural figure before and since. . . . [In fact,] Shakespeare is used in China as a means of constructing cultural meaning' (*Shakespeare*: 175, 176).

The paradox of Shakespeare in the New China, however, is that the Chinese have mostly adapted and appropriated the playwright for their own ideological and aesthetic purposes. They have dressed the Bard in various Chinese opera styles, forced him to be an apologist for Marxism–Leninism–Mao Zedong Thought, celebrated his lesser plays, neglected several of his masterpieces, excised sex, religion, and contrary politics from his texts, added to them, and at times simplified, corrupted, or misunderstood his characters and themes. Perhaps more than any other nation, China has used a great artist to forward its own ideology rather than meet him on his own ground. Shakespeare in China is, in a sense, like Shylock in Venice, a sometimes useful but potentially dangerous 'fly through the open door' that can threaten to disrupt cultural and political values. In earlier times, Shakespeare was one symbol of needed reform in Chinese drama and a response to xenophobic isolationism. More recently, however, Shakespeare, like Shylock, has been converted. Now he often serves a favoured ideology. But his assimilation has not been complete. A few brave Chinese scholars, critics, and directors have tested the limits. Let's hope more will do so in the future.

Bibliography

Anikst, Alexander. *Biography of Shakespeare*, trans. An Guoliang. Beijing: Zhongguo xiju chubanshe, 1984.

Atkinson, Brooks. 'The Play', *New York Times*. 18 December 1942: 1, 38.

Barme, Geremie. 'Not Wisely But Too Well – *Othello* in Beijing'. *Chinese Literature* (September 1983): 114–18.

Beijing Review 28:1. 7 January 1985: 45.

Berry, Edward. 'Teaching Shakespeare in China'. *Shakespeare Quarterly* 39:2 (Summer 1988): 212–16.

Bian Zhilin. 'On Translating *Hamlet* into Chinese and on the Chinese Dubbing of the Film Version'. *Shakespeare Studies (China)* 1 (1983): 6–25.

Bohannan, Laura. 'Shakespeare in the Bush'. *Natural History* 75:7 (August–September 1966): 28–33.

Brandon, James R. 'Some Shakespeare(s) in Some Asia(s)'. *Asian Studies Review* 20:3 (April 1997): 1–26.

Brockbank, J. Philip. 'Shakespeare Renaissance in China'. *Shakespeare Quarterly* 39:2 (Summer 1988): 195–203.

Butterfield, Fox. 'The Old Vic Takes "Hamlet" to China', *New York Times*. 25 November 1979.

Byron, George Gordon (Lord). *'The Flesh is Frail': Byron's Letters and Journals 6 (1818–19)*, ed. Leslie A. Marchand. Cambridge, MA.: Harvard University Press, 1976.

Cao Shujun and Sun Fuliang. *Shashibiya zai Zhongguo wutaishang* [*Shakespeare on the Chinese Stage*]. Harbin: Harbin chubanshe, 1989.

Cao [Tsao] Weifeng. 'Shakespeare in China'. *China Reconstructs* 4 (July 1955).
—— 'Shakespeare in China'. *Wenyi yuebao* [*Art and Literature Monthly*] (April 1954): 29–34.
Cao Xueqin. *The Story of the Stone*, trans. David Hawkes and John Minford, 5 vols. Harmondsworth: Penguin, 1973–86.
—— *A Dream of Red Mansions* [*Hongloumeng*], trans. Yang Hsien-yi and Gladys Yang, 3 vols. Beijing: Foreign Languages Press, 1978–80.
Cao Yu. 'Inaugural Observations'. *Shakespeare Studies* (*China*) 1 (1983): 1–4.
—— 'Learn From Shakespeare' [*Xiang Shashibiya xuexi*]. *Shakespeare Studies* (*China*) 1. Reprinted from *People's Daily* [*Renmin ribao*] (5 April 1983).
Chan, Mimi. 'Figurative Language in Shakespeare: The Hong Kong Student's Response', *New Studies in Shakespeare*, ed. Ruan Shen. Wuchang: Wuhan University Press, 1994: 252–63.
Chang Chen-Hsien. 'Shakespeare in China.' M.A. thesis: University of Birmingham, UK, 1951.
—— 'Shakespeare in China', *Shakespeare Survey 6*, ed. Allardyce Nicoll. Cambridge: Cambridge University Press, 1953: 112–16.
Chen Jia. 'Shakespeare's Political Views Revealed in His Historical Plays', *Shakespeare Criticism in China*, ed. Meng Xianqiang. Changchun: Jilin Education Press, 1991: 141–58.
Chu, Pingyi. 'Taoistic Ideas in the Works of Shakespeare'. *Studies in English Literature and Linguistics* 4 (1980): 87–109.
Chu, Rudolph J. 'Shakespeare in China: Translations and Translators'. *Tamkang Review* 1:2 (October 1970): 155–81.
Confucius. *The Analects*, trans. D.C. Lau. Harmondsworth: Penguin Books, 1979.

Diamond, Catherine. '*Kingdom of Desire*: The Three Faces of *Macbeth*'. *Asian Theatre Journal* 11:1 (1994): 114–33.
Dong Run. 'Talks on Shakespeare's Poetic Genre (1917–1918)', *Shakespeare Criticism in China*, ed. Meng Xianqiang. Changchun: Jilin Education Press, 1991: 52–57.

Eliot, T.S. 'Tradition and the Individual Talent', *The Sacred Wood*. London: University Paperbacks, 1960: 47–59.
Eoyang, Eugene Chen. 'From the Imperial to the Empirical: Teaching English in Hong Kong', *Profession 2000*, ed. Phyllis Franklin. New York: The Modern Language Association of America, 2000: 62–74.
Evening Standard (London). 11 June 1979.

Fan Shen. 'Shakespeare in China: *The Merchant of Venice*'. *Asian Theatre Journal* 5:1 (1988): 23–37.

Fang Ping. *New Complete Works of William Shakespeare [Xin Shashibiya quanji]*, 12 vols. Hubei: Hubei Educational Publishing House, 1999.

——— *New Complete Works of William Shakespeare*. Taibei: Owl Publishing House, 2000.

Fei, Faye Chunfang. *Chinese Theories of Theatre and Performance from Confucius to the Present*. Ann Arbor: University of Michigan Press, 1999.

Fung Yulan. *A Short History of Chinese Philosophy*. New York: Macmillan, 1960.

Greenblatt, Stephen. 'China: Visiting Rites'. *Raritan* 2:4 (1983): 19.

Guillain, Robert. *When China Wakes*. New York: Walker, 1965.

He Qixin. 'China's Shakespeare'. *Shakespeare Quarterly* 37:2 (Summer 1986): 149–59.

——— 'Major Trends of Shakespeare Criticism in China.' *Proceedings of the Patristic, Mediaeval and Renaissance Conference* [at Villanova University] 9 (1984): 95–101.

——— 'On Translating Shakespeare into Chinese'. M.A. thesis: University of Akron, Ohio, 1984.

——— 'Shakespeare Through Chinese Eyes'. Ph.D. dissertation. Kent State University, 1986. [Abbr. *STCE* in text.]

——— 'Teaching Shakespeare in Chinese Universities', *Chinese Shakespeare Yearbook, 1994*, ed. Meng Xianqiang. Changchun: Northeast Normal University Press, 1995: 211–24.

He Xianglin. 'Some Comments on Zhu Shenghao's Translation of Shakespeare's Plays', *Essays on Shakespeare*, ed. He Xianglin. Xian: Shaanxi People's Publishing House, 1982: 294–314.

Hessler, Peter. *The New Yorker*. 13 November 2000: 1–10.

Ho Hsiang-Lin. 'Shakespeare in China'. *The Comparatist* 13 (1989): 11–21.

Hsu, Kai-yu. *The Chinese Literary Scene: A Writer's Visit to the People's Republic*. New York: Vintage, 1975.

Huang Zuolin. 'Producing Shakespeare in China'. *Chinese Literature* 4 (Winter 1984): 202–11.

Illustrated London News. 'Shakespeare in China: "Romeo and Juliet" Performed in Peking'. 13 October 1956: 615.

'Interview, Jiang Zemin.' *Time*. 27 October 1997: 58.
'Interview, Lois Wheeler Snow.' *Time*. 11 June 2001: 23.

Jaynes, Nanette. 'Taming the Taiwanese Shrew: *Kiss Me Nana* at the Godot Theatre.' *Shakespeare Yearbook 10*, ed. Holger Klein. Lewiston, NY: Edwin Mellen Press, 1999: 490–507.

Lau, D.C. 'Introduction' to *The Analects* of Confucius. Harmondsworth: Penguin Books, 1979.

Levith, Murray J. *Shakespeare's Italian Settings and Plays*. New York: St. Martin's, 1989.

—— 'Shakespeare's *Merchant* and Marlowe's Other Play', *The Merchant of Venice: New Critical Essays*, eds. John W. Mahon and Ellen Macleod Mahon. New York: Routledge, 2002: 95–106.

Li Funing. '*As You Like It*', *Shakespeare Criticism in China*, ed. Meng Xianqiang. Changchun: Jilin Education Press, 1991.

Li Ruru. 'Chinese Traditional Theatre and Shakespeare'. *Asian Theatre Journal* 5:1 (Spring 1988): 38–48.

—— 'Macbeth Becomes Ma Pei: An Odyssey from Scotland to China'. *Theatre Research International* 20:1 (1995): 42–53.

—— 'The Bard in the Middle Kingdom'. *Asian Theatre Journal* 12:1 (Spring 1995): 50–84.

Li Ruru and David Jiang. 'The 1994 Shanghai International Shakespeare Festival: An Update on the Bard in Cathay'. *Asian Theatre Journal* 14 (1997): 93–119.

Liang Shiqiu, trans. *Complete Works of William Shakespeare* [*Shashibiya quanji*], 12 vols. Taibei: Far East Press, 1967.

—— 'Li-yen', *Bao-feng-yu* [*The Tempest*], trans. Liang Shiqiu. Taipei: Commercial Press, 1974.

—— 'The Significance of *The Merchant of Venice*', *Shakespeare Criticism in China*, ed. Meng Xianqiang. Changchun: Jilin Education Press, 1991: 57–62.

Louie, Kam. *Critiques of Confucius in Contemporary China*. Hong Kong: The Chinese University Press, 1980.

Lu Gusun. 'Hamlet Across Space and Time', *Shakespeare Survey 36*, ed. Stanley Wells. Cambridge: Cambridge University Press, 1983: 53–56.

—— 'Reflections After the Curtainfall'. *Shakespeare Studies (China)* 1: 18–42.

Lu Xun [Hsun]. 'Literature and Sweat', *Lu Hsun: Writing for the Revolution.* San Francisco: Red Sun Publishers, 1976.

Mao Dun [Wei Ming]. 'Shakespeare and Realism'. *Wenshi [Literature and History]* 1:3 (1934): 81–83.

Mao Tse-Tung [Zedong]. *Poems of Mao Tse-tung*, trans. Hualing Nieh Engle and Paul Engle. New York: Dell, 1972.

—— 'On the Correct Handling of Contradictions Among the People', *Communist China, 1955–1959: Policy Documents With Analysis.* Cambridge, MA: Harvard University Press, 1962: 273–94.

—— 'Talk to the Music Workers', *Mao Tse-tung on Art and Literature.* Peking: Foreign Languages Press, 1960: 84–90.

—— 'Talks at the Yenan Forum on Art and Literature', *Selected Works 4 (1941–1945).* New York: International Publishers, 1956: 63–93.

Marx and Engels on Literature and Art, eds. Lee Baxandall and Stefan Thorowski. St. Louis: Telos Press, 1983.

Marx, Karl and Frederick Engels. *Collected Works.* New York: International Publishers, 1975: vols. 1–3.

Meng Xianqiang. *A Historical Survey of Shakespeare in China*, trans. Mason Y.H. Wang and Murray J. Levith. Changchun: Shakespeare Research Centre of Northeast Normal University, 1996.

——, ed. *Shakespeare Criticism in China.* Changchun: Jilin Education Press, 1991.

Montaigne. *The Essayes of Montaigne*, trans. John Florio. New York: The Modern Library, 1900.

Morozov, Mikhail. 'On the Dynamism of Shakespeare's Characters', *Shakespeare in the Soviet Union: A Collection of Articles*, trans. Avril Pyman, eds. Roman Samarin and Alexander Nikolyukin. Moscow, 1966: 113–40.

Perng, Ching-Hsi. 'Chinese *Hamlets*: A Centenary Review'. Lecture: September 2000.

—— Response to author's questionnaire: March 2001.

Qiu Ke'an. 'Annotated *Hamlet* Available', *China Daily.* 5 February 1985: 5, 6.

The Riverside Shakespeare, 2nd edn textual eds. G. Blakemore Evans and J.J.M. Tobin. Boston: Houghton Mifflin, 1997.

Said, Edward. *Orientalism*. New York: Pantheon, 1978.

Schoenhols, Michael, ed. *China's Cultural Revolution, 1966–1969: Not a Dinner Party*. Armonk, NY: M.E. Sharpe, 1996.

Schram, Stuart, ed. *Chairman Mao Talks to the People: Talks and Letters, 1956–1971*, trans. John Chinnery and Tieyun. New York: Pantheon, 1974: 84–90.

Smirnov, Alexander. 'Shakespeare: A Marxist Interpretation', *Approaches to Shakespeare*, ed. Norman Rabkin. New York: McGraw–Hill, 1964: 160–71.

Snow, Lois Wheeler. *China on Stage: An American Actress in the People's Republic*. New York: Vintage Books, 1973.

Sontag, Susan. *On Photography*. New York: Anchor Books, 1990.

Spence, Jonathan. *The Search for Modern China*. New York: Norton, 1990.

Stanley, Audrey. 'The 1994 International Shakespeare Festival'. *Shakespeare Quarterly* 49 (Spring 1996): 72–80.

Sun Dayu. 'Preface', *Shakespeare Criticism in China*, ed. Meng Xianqiang. Changchun: Jilin Education Press, 1991: 111–20.

Sun Jiaxiu. 'Our Chinese *King Lear–Li Ya Wang*', *Wen Yuan* 3, *Studies in Language, Literature, and Culture*, ed. Wang Zuoliang. Beijing: Foreign Language Teaching and Research Press, 1991: 74–81.

Tagore, Amitendranath. *Literary Debates in Modern China, 1918–1937*. Tokyo: The Centre for East Asian Cultural Studies, 1967.

Tian Han, trans. *Hamlet*. Shanghai: Zhonghau Bookstore, 1922.

Timon of Athens by William Shakespeare. ed. H.J. Oliver. London: Methuen, 1959.

Twelfth Night by William Shakespeare. eds. Roger Warren and Stanley Wells. Oxford: Oxford University Press, 1994.

Tsai Chin. 'Teaching and Directing in China: Chinese Theatre Revisited'. *Asian Theatre Journal* 3:1 (1986): 118–31.

Vulpi, Frank. 'A Taoist Reading of *King Lear*'. *Chinese Culture* 33:2 (September 1992): 45–51.

Wakeman, Carolyn. '*Measure for Measure* On the Chinese Stage'. *Shakespeare Quarterly* 33:4 (Winter 1982): 499–502.

Wang, Shuhua. 'Politics into Play: Shakespeare in Twentieth-Century China'. Ph.D. dissertation: The Pennsylvania State University, 1993.

Wang Zuoliang, ed. *Preliminary Essays on Shakespeare – and Shakespeare in China*. Chongqing: Chongqing chubanshe, 1991.

Webb, Barry. *Edmund Blunden: A Biography*. New Haven: Yale University Press, 1990.

White, R.S. 'Marx and Shakespeare', *Shakespeare Survey 45*, ed. Stanley Wells. Cambridge: Cambridge University Press, 1993: 89–101.

Wilkinson, J. Norman. 'Shakespeare in China'. *New England Theatre Journal* 2:1 (1991): 39–58.

Wilson, Patricia. '. . . A Real Interpreter Who Can Act'. *Chinese Literature* 3 (March 1982): 55–72.

Wong, Dorothy. ' "Domination by Consent": A Study of Shakespeare in Hong Kong', eds. Theo D'haen and Patricia Krus. *Studies in Comparative Literature* 26:2 (Amsterdam: Rodopi, 2000): 43–56.

Wong, Dorothy Wai Yi. 'Shakespeare in Hong Kong: Transplantation and Transposition'. M.Phil. thesis. Hong Kong Baptist University, 1995.

Wu, John C.H. 'Shakespeare as a Taoist'. *T'ien Hsia Monthly* 3 (1936): 116–36.

Yang, Daniel S.P. 'Materials on *Dream* for Jay Halio'. Unpublished paper.
—— 'Shakespeare at Hong Kong Repertory Theatre', *Shakespeare in China: Performance and Perspectives – A Collection of Theses*. Shanghai: Shanghai Theatre Academy, 1999: 75–85.

Yang Hengsheng. *China Today* 35:7 (July 1986): 41–43.

Yang, Hui, trans. 'On *Timon of Athens*', ed. Meng Xianqiang. *Shakespeare Criticism in China*. Changchun: Jilin Education Press, 1991.

Yang Lingui. 'New Chinese Approaches to Shakespeare: An International Shakespeare Conference in Central China'. *Shakespeare Newsletter* (Fall 1993): 56.
—— '1994 International Shakespeare Festival'. *Shakespeare Newsletter* (Winter 1994): 79.
—— 'Chinese Commemorate Translator of Shakespeare'. *Shakespeare Newsletter* (Summer 1992): 22.
—— 'Major Approaches to Shakespeare in the 90's'. Shakespeare Association of America Conference, 2000.

Yang Zhouhan. '*King Lear* Metamorphosed'. *Comparative Literature* 39 (1987): 256–63.
—— 'The Mirror and the Jigsaw: A Major Difference between Current Chinese and Western Critical Attitudes'. *Representations* 1:4 (1983): 101–107.

Yu Weijie. *The Dramatic Touch of Difference: Theatre Own and Foreign*, eds. Erika Fischer-Lichte, Josephine Riley and Michael Gissenwehrer. Tubingen: Gunter Narr, 1990: 161–67.

Zha Peide and Tian Jia. 'Shakespeare and Traditional Chinese Operas'. *Shakespeare Quarterly* 39:2 (Summer 1988): 204–11.

Zhang Xiaoyang. *Shakespeare in China: A Comparative Study of Two Traditions and Cultures*. Newark: University of Delaware Press, 1996.

Zhu Shenghao, trans. *Complete Works of Shakespeare* [*Shashibiya quanji*], 11 vols. Beijing: People's Publishing House, 1978.

—— 'Translator's Preface' to *The Complete Works of Shakespeare*. Shanghai: Shijie shiju, 1947: 1–3.

Index

Illustrations are noted by page numbers in **bold** type